REST
In the Shadow of the
ALMIGHTY

Thank you so
much for inviting me to
speak at your church. May
you continue to grow in Grace.

Grace,

03/22/14

Rest in the Shadow of the Almighty
Discover the Joy that is Found Living
Under the Sovereignty of God

ISBN-13: 978-1456342906
ISBN-10: 1456342908

Printed in the United States of America

REST

In the Shadow of the

ALMIGHTY

Discover the Joy that is Found Living
Under the Sovereignty of God

by

Daniel R. Ledwith

This book is dedicated to
Charles "Tremendous" Jones.

TABLE OF CONTENTS

ACKNOWLEDGMENTS

No achievement worth striving for is ever done alone. This book has passed through many hands and I have had much help, counsel, and support along the way.

First, I want to acknowledge my parents whose support and guidance for me and to me has been invaluable. I would also like to give special thanks to First Parish Congregational Church for their support and willingness to put up with me as I thought through, preached, and taught on much of the contents of this book.

My friend and mentor Charlie "Tremendous" Jones was a tremendous (pun definitely intended) help and encouragement to me. I am so grateful for the friendship that we had. Without his counsel this book could not have been done. The same holds true for my friends Earl Sheaff and Steve Poole.

I also need to thank Mark Panagakis, the owner of Mark's Smoke Shop in Wakefield, MA, for making it possible for me to enjoy a cigar while writing this book in his shop.

More than any person, I need to thank my wife Mandi for giving me the freedom to do what it took to pull this manuscript together. It could not have happened without her being willing to make the sacrifices she did.

Most importantly I want to thank God for being my Lord, my Savior, my help, and my friend. This book was written to glorify Him and to help its readers to increase their joy and wonder in our Sovereign God. I thank Him for giving me the opportunity to serve Him through this book.

PSALM 91

Those who live in the shelter of the Most High will find rest in the shadow of the Almighty.

This I declare about the LORD: He alone is my refuge, my place of safety; he is my God, and I trust him.

For he will rescue you from every trap and protect you from deadly disease.

He will cover you with his feathers. He will shelter you with his wings. His faithful promises are your armor and protection.

Do not be afraid of the terrors of the night, nor the arrow that flies in the day.

Do not dread the disease that stalks in darkness, nor the disaster that strikes at midday.

Though a thousand fall at your side, though ten thousand are dying around you, these evils will not touch you.

Just open your eyes, and see how the wicked are punished. If you make the LORD your refuge, if you make the Most High your shelter, no evil will conquer you; no plague will come near your home. For he will order his angels to protect you wherever you go.

They will hold you up with their hands so you won't even hurt your foot on a stone. You will trample upon lions and cobras; you will crush fierce lions and serpents under your feet!

The LORD says, "I will rescue those who love me. I will protect those who trust in my name. When they call on me, I will answer; I will be with them in trouble. I will rescue and honor them. I will reward them with a long life and give them my salvation."

THE PROMISE

Those who live in the shelter of the Most High will find rest in the shadow of the Almighty.

PSALM 91:1

It is not enough to hear about Jesus: mere hearing may tune the harp, but the fingers of living faith must create the music. If you have seen Jesus with the God-giving sight of faith, suffer no cobwebs to linger among the harp strings, but loud to the praise of sovereign grace, awake your psaltery and harp.

C.H. SPURGEON, *MORNING AND EVENING*,
EVENING JANUARY 28

Do you have a love-hate relationship with God's sovereignty, His right and power to control His creation? Many Christians have this struggle. The love side is that we don't have any trouble accepting that God is in control when things are going our way. In seasons of blessing we are eager to believe that God is in control of everything.

But then there's the hate side. When we start thinking about our problems, challenges, and all the evil in the world, we almost instinctively start to back off and exclaim that God is not in control of everything. When bad things happen, we seem automatically to question just how far God's control goes.

This love-hate relationship penetrates all the way down into our freedom of choice. We are very free with ascribing our choices and decisions to the control and influence of God when good things happen as the result of our decisions. But when we make bad or hurtful decisions, or when people do horrible things, we wonder if we really want to say that God is sovereign in all of the choices we make.

It seems that deep down we fear that there are shadows in the Light... that God isn't as in control of the universe as the Bible wants us to believe He is. So we spend our time focused on the things about God that don't trouble us so much like His love, goodness, grace, trustworthiness and faithfulness.

What I have been learning is that when we try to relate to God apart from understanding this biblical characteristic of the sovereignty of God, we pull the rug out from under our faith in God's promises to be loving, good, gracious, trustworthy, and faithful to us. As a result we often end up being hounded or even imprisoned by shame, depression, guilt, anxiety, and fear.

The Bible is full of exhortations, stories, parables, teaching, proverbs, and promises that were given by God to speak directly to us about those problems. He paid for our release at the cross. Yet many Christians still live in cages with bars made of depression, fear, anxiety, guilt, and shame. Why is that?

At first sight, this might not seem like a big deal. After all, these are very familiar problems to just about everyone. People have been struggling with every one of those problems since the fall of Adam and Eve.

There are admittedly many legitimate reasons why people struggle with each of those issues. But one reason which lies at the root of our struggles is our trouble believing in God's sovereignty. The key that unlocks the door to God's promises of rest, freedom, peace and joy is realizing that

God is not just Mighty, but Almighty!

One of great promises in the Bible is Psalm 91. In verse 1 of this Psalm, God gives an amazing promise,

> Those who live in the shelter of the Most High will find rest in the shadow of the Almighty.

I have been learning that "rest" is one of the most elusive treasures we seek. We are constantly on the go and on the job. Rest is something we talk about, but something we rarely experience. God wants us to know that the rest He offers is real and not a fantasy, and it is found under the shadow of the Most High.

The psalmist declares the grounds for taking and trusting this promise in verses 2-4.

> This I declare about the LORD: He alone is my refuge, my place of safety; he is my God, and I trust him. For he will rescue you from every trap and protect you from deadly disease. He will cover you with his feathers. He will shelter you with his wings. His faithful promises are your armor and protection.

The reason we can take shelter in God's love and grace and rest under His shadow is that He is faithful to His promises. You can count on God to deliver because there is nothing that can stop Him from keeping His word. God wants you to know that His promises are so strong and dependable that you can look at them as body armor! He is Almighty! He is sovereign!

The remaining 11 verses paint a clear picture of the kind of rest that is found when we rest under the shadow of the Almighty. First we are told that when we take shelter in the shadow of the Most High we will find rest from anxiety and worry.

Do not be afraid of the terrors of the night, nor the arrow that flies in the day. Do not dread the disease that stalks in darkness, nor the disaster that strikes at midday.

Next we are told that we will find rest from depression. No matter what circumstances we might find ourselves in, nothing can defeat us and take us out of His care.

Though a thousand fall at your side, though ten thousand are dying around you, these evils will not touch you. Just open your eyes, and see how the wicked are punished. If you make the LORD your refuge, if you make the Most High your shelter, no evil will conquer you; no plague will come near your home. For he will order his angels to protect you wherever you go. They will hold you up with their hands so you won't even hurt your foot on a stone.

When we are living under the shadow of the Almighty we will find rest from the fear of failure.

You will trample upon lions and cobras; you will crush fierce lions and serpents under your feet!

There is also rest from shame because He treats us with honor and assures us we are the recipients of His special love and care.

The LORD says, "I will rescue those who love me. I will protect those who trust in my name. When they call on me, I will answer; I will be with them in trouble. I will rescue and honor them."

And last we are assured that when we come to live in the shelter of God, we will find rest from guilt through His salvation that comes with total forgiveness.

I will reward them with a long life and give them my
salvation.

The rest that Christ purchased for us is anchored in the
sovereignty of God. Because God is sovereign we find rest
from depression, anxiety, fear of failure, guilt, and shame.
Because God is sovereign we find the freedom to live a life
full of joy, to let go of our past, have hope for the future,
live boldly, and love passionately.

Discussions of sovereignty have been largely relegated to
debates on predestination, the problem of evil, and the like.
Far from being a clear doctrine with relevant implications
pointing to how we live and grow in God's grace on a daily
basis, it has been left by many Christians as an old and
irrelevant doctrine that is not necessary for Christian living
outside of seminaries.

We cannot blame the members of our churches for this.
The fault lies with us pastors, teachers, and leaders of the
Church. We have not spent the time to adequately
communicate to the person in the pew (or even to the
seminary student) the practical, down to earth, daily impact
that the sovereignty of God has on every believer and on
the Church in general.

If how we think about God's sovereignty can help us to
live a life full of joy, to let go of our past, have hope for the
future, live boldly, and love passionately, then sovereignty is
not one of those dry mental exercises with no value other
than entertaining academics. This means sovereignty is as
practical, even basic to the health of the Christian as
knowing God's love, grace, and forgiveness.

The aim of this book is to encourage you not only to
accept the sovereignty of God, but to love it, to praise God
for it, and to live your life in the confidence of it! We will

find the guarantee of the rest and freedom Christ has for us in one place—under the shadow of the Almighty.

In chapter 1, we will take a clear and honest look at what the Bible says about the sovereignty of God in order to convince you that God is indeed completely in control of everything that happens in this world, and therefore He is also able to be absolutely faithful in keeping all His promises.

The remaining chapters describe how God's sovereignty impacts us every day of our lives by securing the promises of God to give us rest from depression, anxiety, fear, guilt, and shame, and to give us the freedom to live with joy, to make peace with our past, to have confident hope, to live boldly, and to love God with all our heart, soul, mind, and strength, and to love our neighbor as ourselves.

Each chapter concludes with three helpful tools. They will help you bring the joy of knowing God's sovereignty into your life, family, and church. The first is under the heading, *Freedom Under Sovereignty Means*. This is a summary of the main ideas in the chapter, and a memory verse that focuses on the theme of the chapter.

The section *Learning to Live Under Sovereignty* contains study questions for each chapter to help you not only think through the chapter, but to guide and encourage you to bring the truth of the sovereignty of God deep into your heart and how you live your life. These questions can be used for personal study or in going through the book in a small group. These are the same questions we use when teaching through this book at my church.

Lastly, *Cultivating Freedom Under Sovereignty* is a tool for pastors and leaders where I offer some guiding thoughts and concrete ideas that you can use to begin to implement the truth about God's sovereignty into your church, small group, family and ministry.

May our Sovereign God bless you and may your love for Him and amazement in Him increase as you discover the joy that comes from living under the sovereignty of God.

Chapter 1

THE GROUND OF THE PROMISE

This I declare about the LORD: He alone is my refuge, my place of safety; he is my God, and I trust him. For he will rescue you from every trap and protect you from deadly disease. He will cover you with his feathers. He will shelter you with his wings. His faithful promises are your armor and protection.

PSALM 91:2-4

Many a rock might be escaped, if we would let our Father take the helm; many a shoal or quicksand we might well avoid, if we would leave to his sovereign will to choose and to command.

C.H. SPURGEON, *MORNING AND EVENING*,
MORNING FEBRUARY 9

How do you respond when things don't go your way? How do you respond in a crisis? Do you get anxious and fall apart? Do you become discouraged and depressed? Do you tend to think that all this trouble is because you are guilty of something and God has made it His business to severely punish you for it?

How you think and what you believe are directly connected to how you act. We can take that one step further: How you think and what you believe *about God* are directly connected to how you act.

In the chapters ahead we are going to think through some of the spiritual defenses and helps we have against depression, anxiety, fear of failure, chronic feelings of guilt, and shame when we are planted in the rich soil of God's sovereignty. But before we do, we need to have a clear, biblically informed idea of God's sovereignty and what it means. We need a sovereign God. Sovereignty is necessary for us to have the freedom we are promised in Christ.

It seems that an informed and sincere understanding of sovereignty is missing from our understanding of God today. It's missing for any number of reasons, but you have probably found that problems with sovereignty basically fit into one of these two concerns:

We don't like how some realities such as war, murder, rape, cancer, and natural disasters make God look. They make us question God's goodness, love, and wisdom.

We don't like the thought that our choices and decisions are somehow under God's control. It seems to take away the essence of our free will.

In light of concerns like these, the great majority of Christians today would rather say God is not in control of everything. But what has happened as a result? Ironically, one of the most important truths we need in order to work through times of pain and suffering and the consequences of our choices is the conviction that God is in complete and total control of His creation. To believe otherwise is to say that there are some things that are beyond God's power to redeem or repair.

I had a conversation with a parent in my office who shared with me that their teenage son had recently attempted suicide. This parent was in the middle of a very tough time. His marriage was not doing well and hadn't been for a long time. If they could not work out their problems soon, divorce seemed inevitable. "I just don't get it," this parent told me, "Why would my kid want to die?

We are active in our church, he's in the youth group. He knows that Jesus is the answer."

The problem was that their teen was not getting the idea that "Jesus was the answer" from his parents. Jesus apparently did not have enough power or influence to save their marriage. The God they believed in was not big enough to solve their marriage problems. So why should their son trust God with his own problems, let alone his soul?

I once heard Henry Blackaby say that in all his tenure as a pastor he only had one couple get divorced! When he was asked how he did it he exclaimed that he simply believed that the God who created the universe from nothing was wise enough to fix a marriage. How you think and what you believe about God is directly connected to how you act.

WHAT DOES SOVEREIGNTY MEAN?

The definition of sovereignty in Webster's Dictionary is "supreme power especially over a body politic" and "freedom from external control." When we say that God is sovereign we are saying that He has supreme control over the creation and that He Himself is free from any external control or influence of a greater authority.

Jonathan Edwards, the great American pastor and theologian of the 18th century, wrote a comprehensive explanation of God's sovereignty in his book, *Freedom of the Will*:

> The sovereignty of God is his ability and authority to do whatever pleases him; whereby "he doth according to his will in the armies of heaven, and amongst the inhabitants of the earth; and none can stay his hand, or say unto him, What dost thou?" [Daniel 4:35]. The following things belong to the

sovereignty of God: viz.

(1.) Supreme, universal, and infinite power: whereby he is able to do what he pleases...

(2.) That he has supreme authority; absolute and most perfect right to do what he wills, without subjection to any superior authority, or any derivation of authority from any other [authority]... (3.) That his will is supreme, underived, and independent on any thing without himself; being in every thing determined by his own counsel, having no other rule but his own wisdom...

(4.) That his wisdom, which determines his will, is supreme, perfect, underived, self-sufficient, and independent... It is the glory and greatness of the Divine Sovereign, that God's will is determined by his own infinite, all-sufficient wisdom in every thing; and in nothing at all is either directed by any inferior wisdom, or by no wisdom; whereby it would become senseless arbitrariness, determining and acting without reason, design, or end.[1]

Sovereignty means God is in control. It means that "God is in the heavens and He does as He wishes" (Psalms 115:3).

There can be no doubt that the Bible claims that God is sovereign. More than 280 times throughout the Bible it addresses God with the title "Sovereign Lord." To put that in perspective, consider that the Bible refers to God as sovereign more than it does any other attribute!

HOW FAR DOES GOD'S SOVEREIGNTY GO?

Oswald Chambers said, "God is never in a panic, nothing can be done that He is not absolute Master of, and no one in earth or heaven can shut a door He has opened, nor open a door He has shut." God is in complete and total control of everything that happens in all that He has created. He is in control of all things in heaven and all things on earth. It is absolutely astounding to see the extent of God's control that is ascribed to Him throughout the Bible. Let's take a bird's eye view of how the Bible describes the sovereignty of God.

GOD IS SOVEREIGN OVER NATURE

He creates, preserves, and brings to an end everything in the universe as He pleases. This is made clear from the opening chapters of Genesis where He creates heaven and earth from nothing, through the final chapters of Revelation when He creates a new heaven and a new earth. God is sovereign over all the animals in creation. Jesus said in Matthew 10:29, "Not even a sparrow, worth only half a penny, can fall to the ground without your Father knowing it."

God can command the animals to do as He wills. He commanded ravens to bring Elijah bread and meat in 1 Kings 17:4-6. He gave a donkey the ability to speak to its rider in Numbers 22:28. He commanded a giant fish to swallow Jonah (Jonah 1:17) and directed the fish to spit him back up on land (Jonah 2:10). God directed a flock of quail to land in the Israelites' camp for food (Exodus 16:11-13). He used poisonous snakes to punish the Israelites in the desert in Numbers 21:6. He directed all the animals He wanted to come to Noah and get on the ark (Genesis 7:9). God commanded frogs, gnats, flies, and locusts, to curse the Egyptians (Exodus 8, 10). God caused all the Egyptian livestock to die, but kept Israel's livestock alive and well (Exodus 9). He caused a plant to grow to shade His prophet Jonah and commanded a worm to eat the plant (Jonah 4).

Jesus commanded a fig tree to wither and it did (Matthew 21:19).

He can even control the rising and setting of the sun and the stars (Joshua 10:12-14, Job 9:7). God says in Isaiah 50:2-3, "I can speak to the sea and make it dry! I can turn rivers into deserts covered with dying fish. I am the one who sends darkness out across the skies, bringing it to a state of mourning." God is completely sovereign over all His creation.

GOD IS SOVEREIGN OVER THE WEATHER

The Bible says that lightning, hail, snow, storms, wind and weather obey Him (Psalms 148:8). Jesus could stop storms with a word (Mark 4:39). God withheld rain when He was asked by Elijah (1 Kings 17:1) and made it rain when Elijah asked three and a half years later (1 Kings 18:44).

GOD IS SOVEREIGN OVER NATURAL DISASTER

God rained burning sulfur on Sodom and Gomorrah (Genesis 19:23). He sent a hail and lightning storm down on Egypt in Exodus 9:23. God caused earthquakes to aid the Israelites in battle (1 Samuel 14:15). Job 36:33 says the storm and thunder announce God's presence and anger. God sent the storm to threaten the ship that carried Jonah as he attempted to flee from the presence of the Lord (Jonah 1:4). God sent a whirlwind to carry Elijah up to heaven (2 Kings 2:11). In Isaiah 29:6 God says, "In an instant, I, the LORD Almighty, will come against them with thunder and earthquake and great noise, with whirlwind and storm and consuming fire." Nineteen times throughout the Bible God claims to be responsible for or promises to bring famine.

GOD IS SOVEREIGN OVER DISEASE

The Bible says that God in His sovereignty brings disease. God says He can bring "deadly disease" in Deuteronomy 32:24. He brought disease upon Pharaoh and Abimelek for taking Abraham's wife into their harems (Genesis 12:17, 20:17). He brought boils onto the Egyptians for not letting the Israelites go (Exodus 9:10). He allowed Satan to inflict Job with boils from head to foot (Job 2:7).

The Bible also says that God in His sovereignty heals and takes away diseases. God healed Pharaoh and Abimelek of the diseases He sent on them and their families when Abraham prayed for their healing. He healed Hezekiah of a terminal illness in 2 Kings 20:5. Jesus healed people of blindness, bleeding, demon possession, and paralysis. Matthew 4:23-24 says,

> Jesus traveled throughout Galilee teaching in the synagogues, preaching everywhere the Good News about the Kingdom. And he healed people who had every kind of sickness and disease. News about him spread far beyond the borders of Galilee so that the sick were soon coming to be healed from as far away as Syria. And whatever their illness and pain, or if they were possessed by demons, or were epileptics, or were paralyzed—he healed them all.

GOD IS SOVEREIGN OVER LIFE AND DEATH

He caused Sarah to become pregnant for the first time in her life at ninety years of age (Genesis 21:1-2). He caused Hannah to become pregnant with Samuel when she prayed for a son, having not been able to have children for years (1 Samuel 1:20). God decides when every living thing dies (Psalm 139:16). He determines whether people die at all

(Hebrews 11:5). He is sovereign even over death. God answered Elijah's prayer to raise the widow's son from the dead (1 Kings 17:22). Jesus raised people from the dead (Matthew 9:18-26, John 11:44). God raised Eutychus from the dead when Paul prayed for him (Acts 20:10). And, of course, Jesus Himself rose from the dead. In Revelation 1:17-18, Jesus says "I am the First and the Last. I am the living one. I died, but look—I am alive forever and ever! And I hold the keys of death and the grave."

GOD IS SOVEREIGN OVER THE NATIONS

God says in Jeremiah 1:10, "Today I appoint you to stand up against nations and kingdoms. Some you must uproot and tear down, destroy and overthrow. Others you must build up and plant." God called Israel to overthrow the nations living in the Promised Land. He Called Assyria to punish Samaria and called Babylon to punish Judah. In dreams given to Daniel God foretold the fall of Babylon, the rise of Persia, the rise of Greece, and the rise of Rome (Daniel 2:24-45).

GOD IS SOVEREIGN OVER RULERS

He says clearly in Romans 13:1-2 that "all authority comes from God, and those in positions of authority have been placed there by God. So anyone who rebels against authority is rebelling against what God has instituted, and they will be punished." The Bible is full of examples of God's sovereignty over national leaders. He appointed Pharaoh for the express purpose of showing his power and sovereignty over him. He humbled Nebuchadnezzar, the king of Babylon, so that he himself wrote in Daniel 4:34-35,

> After this time had passed, I, Nebuchadnezzar, looked up to heaven. My sanity returned, and I

praised and worshiped the Most High and honored the one who lives forever. His rule is everlasting, and his kingdom is eternal. All the people of the earth are nothing compared to him. He does as he pleases among the angels of heaven and among the people of the earth. No one can stop him or say to him, 'What do you mean by doing these things?'

He foretold that Cyrus, king of Persia, would let Israel return to Jerusalem to rebuild the city and the temple at Persia's expense more than a century before he was ever born and indeed before Persia was even a world power (Isaiah 45:1-13). When Caiaphas the high priest counseled the Pharisees to kill Jesus because it was better for one man to die than the nation, God was speaking through him (John 11:51). When Pilate ordered Jesus flogged and crucified, he was doing what God had said about Jesus' death in the Old Testament prophets (Isaiah 53:5-6). Jesus even told Pilate that he had been given no power other than what God had given him (John 19:11). Acts 17:26 says, "From one man he created all the nations throughout the whole earth. He decided beforehand which should rise and fall, and he determined their boundaries."

GOD IS SOVEREIGN OVER INDIVIDUALS

He is not just sovereign over the influential and the important, He is sovereign over the lives of all people. He is sovereign over our destinies (Esther 4:14, Jeremiah 1:5). He is sovereign over our actions and decisions. Proverbs 20:24 says "The LORD directs our steps." He determines where we go and where we do not go (Acts 16:6). God determines our strengths and weaknesses (1 Corinthians 12:8-10). It is God who determines when we are born and when we die (Psalm 139:16).

GOD IS SOVEREIGN AS THE JUDGE OF THE WORLD

God claims to be the ultimate Judge over all nations and peoples (Psalms 9:8, 96:10-13). He will execute justice and righteousness over the people of the earth (Jeremiah 25:31). Jesus said that He came to judge the world (John 9:39). God's Law was given as the final law to which all people will be accountable (Romans 3:19). God will judge all people according to what they have done respecting His Law (Psalms 62:11-12, Romans 2:5-6). When God judges, His word is final. There is no higher court to which God's judgments can be appealed (Job 31:23, Isaiah 63:5). God declares in Isaiah 43:13 "Yes, and from ancient days I am he. No one can deliver out of my hand. When I act, who can reverse it?" (NIV).

GOD IS SOVEREIGN AS SAVIOR

Grace is His to give or withhold as He chooses. This is most clearly stated in Romans 9:15-16, "For God said to Moses, 'I will show mercy to anyone I choose, and I will show compassion to anyone I choose.' So it is God who decides to show mercy. We can neither choose it nor work for it." When God has decided to save, nothing can snatch a person out of His hand. Jesus said in John 10:28-29, "No one will snatch them away from me, for my Father has given them to me, and he is more powerful than anyone else. So no one can take them from me."

Edwards' summary of what God's sovereignty means is no exaggeration. If we are going to take the Bible as God's revelation about Himself, we can't help but come to the conclusion that God is absolutely sovereign.

This sovereignty can make us uncomfortable and even uncertain about God's goodness, love, and compassion. What about our own free will? Doesn't an absolute sovereign God nullify our free will as human beings?

Whatever we do, our answers to those questions can't downplay the clear reality of God's sovereignty. We shouldn't be afraid to trust in the sovereignty of God because we do not fully understand it. God declares in Isaiah 55:8-9,

> "My thoughts are completely different from yours," says the LORD. "And my ways are far beyond anything you could imagine. For just as the heavens are higher than the earth, so are my ways higher than your ways and my thoughts higher than your thoughts."

Most people do not know how their car works. We know there is an engine, but how many of us can take it apart and put it together again? I am in that group of people that has absolutely no idea how to do that. I know where the oil goes. I know where the windshield washer fluid goes. That's about it. The rest of the engine is beyond me. I know that I need to change the oil, fill the gas tank, and replace the brakes and tires every once in a while. That's all I know.

Yet, despite this obvious lack of understanding of the mechanics of my automobile, I am fully licensed to drive it and use it effectively every day. The truth is I do not need to fully understand everything about how the engine works in order to drive. I know *someone* understands it. I know it makes sense to my mechanic. But just because I don't have the same knowledge of my car that my mechanic does, it doesn't make my car engine any less logical or understandable.

The same is true about God's sovereignty. We don't have all the answers we would like about how sovereignty harmonizes with His other attributes and our free will. But that does not mean that it isn't in harmony with them.

NOT JUST ANY SOVEREIGNTY, BUT HOLY SOVEREIGNTY

The fact that God's sovereignty is in harmony with His other attributes is what makes the characteristic of sovereignty in God so great. Sovereignty by itself is not necessarily a thing worthy of praise. Power and control are worthy of trust or worthy of fear depending on the kind of person exercising them. God's sovereignty is worth our absolute trust because the God who is absolutely sovereign is also absolutely good, loving, and just. God's moral excellence, his holiness is what makes His power and control so wonderful.

A great illustration of this truth is seen in the latest Superman movie, *Superman Returns*. Superman's arch nemesis, Lex Luthor, has been let out of prison and steals crystals from Superman's secret Fortress of Solitude at the North Pole. These crystals that came from Superman's home world of Krypton can create whole continents when they are exposed to water. Lex plans to replace North America with a new continent that he grows from one of these crystals. He almost succeeds. But Superman, of course, proves unstoppable. Superman gets underneath the growing continent and lifts it out of the sea and lifts it into space even as it continues to grow! Lex Luthor looks on while fleeing in a helicopter at his island continent going up into the sky. The look on his face says it all. It says, *Is there anything he can't do? How can I ever win against that kind of power?* The reason we love Superman is because of his character. He stands for truth, justice, and the American way. And *because of that* we love the fact that he is so strong and powerful.

In Romans 8:31-39 Paul crystallizes for us the reason we can be so joyous and confident in our God... and it all ties back to His holy sovereignty.

> If God is for us, who can ever be against us? Since he did not spare even his own Son but gave him up for us all, won't he also give us everything else?
>
> Who dares accuse us whom God has chosen for his own? No one—for God himself has given us right standing with himself. Who then will condemn us? No one—for Christ Jesus died for us and was raised to life for us, and he is sitting in the place of honor at God's right hand, pleading for us.
>
> Can anything ever separate us from Christ's love? Does it mean he no longer loves us if we have trouble or calamity, or are persecuted, or hungry, or destitute, or in danger, or threatened with death? (As the Scriptures say, "For your sake we are killed every day; we are being slaughtered like sheep.") No, despite all these things, overwhelming victory is ours through Christ, who loved us.
>
> And I am convinced that nothing can ever separate us from God's love. Neither death nor life, neither angels nor demons, neither our fears for today nor our worries about tomorrow—not even the powers of hell can separate us from God's love. No power in the sky above or in the earth below—indeed, nothing in all creation will ever be able to separate us from the love of God that is revealed in Christ Jesus our Lord.

There is no reason to ever doubt that God is able to keep His promises. There is no person, no power, no circumstance, and no combination of any of those that can even come close to challenging the power of God the Father Almighty.

In Jeremiah 29:11 God promises, "For I know the plans I have for you," says the LORD. "They are plans for good and not for disaster, to give you a future and a hope." Nothing can keep God from doing all the good He plans for those He loves.

Jesus promised in John 14:14 to provide for us saying, "ask for anything in my name, and I will do it, because the work of the Son brings glory to the Father." Nothing can stop God from providing all that we need in order to do everything He has planned for us to do and to become all He wants us to be in Christ.

Psalm 9:10 says "Those who know your name will trust in you, for you, LORD, have never forsaken those who seek you." Nothing can stop God from hearing or answering our prayers and helping us in our times of need. He will always prove faithful because He is sovereign.

God declares in Isaiah 45:21-22, "there is no other God but me—a just God and a Savior—no, not one! Let all the world look to me for salvation! For I am God; there is no other." Because God is sovereign nothing can take us away from God's grace and forgiveness.

"Nothing in all creation will ever be able to separate us from the love of God that is revealed in Christ Jesus our Lord." Nothing can separate us from His love because God is sovereign.

When we live in the confidence of those promises we experience the freedom that Christ purchased for us at the cross. When we rest in the absolute trustworthiness of those promises we will gladly submit our lives, our ambitions, our dreams, our talents, all that we are and all that we have to the work and power of the Spirit. When we live in the assurance of these promises, we are free to trust God in ways and in situations that we never thought possible.

Let us rejoice in our awesome and sovereign God. Let us rejoice in the fact that He is sovereign! It is because He is sovereign that we can have absolute faith that He will do all that He promises.

FREEDOM UNDER SOVEREIGNTY MEANS

When we say that God is sovereign we are saying that He has supreme control over the creation and that He Himself is free from any external control or influence of a greater authority.

The fact that God's sovereignty is in harmony with His holiness is what makes the characteristic of sovereignty in God so wonderful.

It is because God is sovereign that we can have absolute faith that He will do all that He promises.

VERSE TO REMEMBER

Our God is in the heavens, and he does as he wishes.
Psalm 115:3

LEARNING TO LIVE UNDER SOVEREIGNTY

1. What is the definition of the sovereignty of God?
2. What Bible verses could you use to back up the idea of the sovereignty of God?
3. What makes God's sovereignty worthy of adoration?
4. Do you think Jonathan Edwards' definition of sovereignty fits the biblical description of God's sovereignty, or does it go too far? Why or why not?
5. Why is God's sovereignty necessary for us to have hope in God's promises to us?
6. What are some consequences of not having a God who is sovereign? How might that effect our faith in God?
7. What are some ways you have heard people downplay or water down the sovereignty of God?
8. Psalm 115:3 says, "Our God is in the heavens, and he does as he wishes." Does that comfort you or does that make you question the trustworthiness of the Bible?
9. What excites you the most about the sovereignty of

God? What is the most challenging to you about it?

10. How have you seen the sovereignty of God at work in your own life?

11. How might understanding and trusting in the sovereignty of God help you in your marriage? As a parent? At work? At church?

CULTIVATING FREEDOM UNDER SOVEREIGNTY

As pastors and leaders in the church we need to be teaching that our theology has a profound impact on how we respond to life's problems and challenges. Many Christians do not walk the talk of God's sovereignty in their lives. At the beginning of this chapter I wrote about a conversation I had with a parent who was telling his son that "Jesus is the answer" to life's problems, while at the same time he and his wife were seriously contemplating divorce.

How can you point out to people in your teaching and personal conversation that Christians need to be consistently living out the truth that God reveals about Himself in the Bible?

Consider a sermon series or small group study on all the ways that the Bible teaches that God is sovereign.

Take the time to memorize the verses at the end of each chapter and encourage your leaders or family members to do the same. Print them in your order of worship so people can take them home. If your church uses PowerPoint presentations, put these verses on the screen before worship begins.

C h a p t e r   2

REST FROM ANXIETY

Do not be afraid of the terrors of the night, nor the arrow that flies in the day. Do not dread the disease that stalks in darkness, nor the disaster that strikes at midday.

PSALM 91:5-6

Anxiety makes us doubt God's lovingkindness, and thus our love to him grows cold; we feel mistrust, and thus grieve the Spirit of God, so that our prayers become hindered, our consistent example marred, and our life one of self-seeking. Thus want of confidence in God leads us to wander far from him; but if through simple faith in his promise, we cast each burden as it comes upon him, and are "careful for nothing" because he undertakes to care for us, it will keep us close to him, and strengthen us against much temptation. "Thou wilt keep him in perfect peace whose mind is stayed on thee, because he trusteth in thee."

C.H. SPURGEON, MORNING AND EVENING,
MORNING MAY 26

When you are doing youth ministry, the one thing you really do not want to hear is that someone is seriously hurt or in physical danger. I remember the first time in my ministry that I got that dreaded news. It was at a confirmation retreat. One of the students came running in and told me that one of the girls had collapsed on the floor in the kitchen.

When I got into the kitchen, there was this student on the floor. Her legs were twitching. She was hardly able to breathe. She was unable to sit up, let alone stand up, and unable to talk. Our first thought was that she was having an asthma attack. I remember praying it wasn't a seizure. It turned out (thankfully) that it was neither of those things. It was an anxiety attack.

Webster's Medical Dictionary defines anxiety as "an abnormal and overwhelming sense of apprehension and fear often marked by physiological signs (such as sweating, tension, and increased pulse), by doubt concerning the reality and nature of the threat, and by self-doubt about one's capacity to cope with it."

Anxiety is a feeling of dread that comes from what *might* happen. Anxiety leads you to question God's trustworthiness. It works very hard with urgent thoughts and images of crisis and criticism to remove God's faithfulness from your mind. Anxiety is a fruit of unbelief in the sovereign provision of God. The way to overcome it is to build your faith in God's sovereignty.

Do you know what the most often given command in the Bible is? *Do not be afraid.* Listen to Jesus speak to you and your anxious spirit. In Matthew 6:25-34 He says,

> So I tell you, don't worry about everyday life-whether you have enough food, drink, and clothes. Doesn't life consist of more than food and clothing? Look at the birds. They don't need to plant or harvest or put food in barns because your heavenly Father feeds them. And you are far more valuable to him than they are. Can all your worries add a single

moment to your life? Of course not.

And why worry about your clothes? Look at the lilies and how they grow. They don't work or make their clothing, yet Solomon in all his glory was not dressed as beautifully as they are. And if God cares so wonderfully for flowers that are here today and gone tomorrow, won't he more surely care for you? You have so little faith!

So don't worry about having enough food or drink or clothing. Why be like the pagans who are so deeply concerned about these things? Your heavenly Father already knows all your needs, and he will give you all you need from day to day if you live for him and make the Kingdom of God your primary concern.

So don't worry about tomorrow, for tomorrow will bring its own worries. Today's trouble is enough for today.

Your sovereign God is in control of your future. Four times in that short passage Jesus tells us not to worry. Peter gives us further direction for dealing with anxiety in 1 Peter 5:6-7,

Humble yourselves, therefore, under the mighty hand of God so that at the proper time he may exalt you, casting all your anxieties on him, because he cares for you. (ESV)

BEING HUMBLE

When you are anxious you are not being humble...at least not humble before God. Anxiety comes from a false expectation that *we* should be in control. We need to recognize that we are not expected to be in control of everything. It means submitting to the reality that God is in control and we are His servants. We aren't supposed to be calling the shots. Calling the shots is God's job. Ours is to play the shots that God calls.

BELIEVING THE FACT GOD CARES FOR YOU

Getting free from anxiety means recognizing and submitting to God's mighty hand. That means learning to rest in knowing that God knows what He is doing even when we don't know what He is doing.

You don't need to be anxious because God cares for you. You are important to Him! The Church is important to Him! It is the bride of His Son! When we have needs, we can feel free to bring them to Him. We have his promise that He will listen to us and that He will provide all we need.

One of the reasons that so many Christians struggle with anxiety is because God's plan for us includes bringing us into places where we quickly realize that we don't have what it takes: we don't have the resources, the confidence, the man power, or the finances. He does this because God wants us to see how trustworthy and faithful *He* is. God is not interested in making us feel capable. He is interested in helping us see that He is capable.

This was one of the lessons that Abraham continued to learn throughout his life. Abraham was anxious about how he would be treated in foreign countries because his wife Sarah was so beautiful. So he had a standing agreement with her that she would tell people she was his sister and hide the fact that she was his wife. Twice (that we know of) this got them into trouble because she was taken by kings whose intent was to marry her. But God was watching over her and would not allow her to be taken advantage of. God spoke to these kings in their dreams telling them to honor her and her husband Abraham and to send her back to him. After each of these events, Abraham learned that God was watching over him and was keeping His promise to bless him and make him great.

But even these events were not enough to keep Abraham from becoming anxious about God's promise to provide everything he needed. God promised Abraham that he would be the father of so many descendants that they would outnumber the stars in the sky and the grains of sand on the seashore. Yet after eleven years from the time this promise was first given, Abraham and Sarah still had no children. Abraham was now 86 years old. Sarah was 76. Things did not look like God was planning to give Abraham a single son of his own with Sarah. But instead of "casting their anxieties on Him" they concluded that maybe God was going to work in other ways. So Sarah came to Abraham with a proposition:

> So Sarai said to Abram, "The LORD has prevented me from having children. Go and sleep with my servant. Perhaps I can have children through her." And Abram agreed with Sarai's proposal (Genesis 16:2).

Abraham and Sarah were anxious. They were worried that they had misunderstood or missed some opportunity and so believed that God was not going to be able to give them a son together.

Could you blame them? They were pretty well convinced that they were both beyond childbearing age. They had never in their married life been able to have kids. It had been over a decade since God had last promised to give them children. So they agreed to allow Sarah's servant Hagar act as a surrogate mother. The plan worked, and Hagar became pregnant.

That is what we tend to do when we get anxious; we often end up taking things into our own hands. When we feel like we need to help God out, we end up causing ourselves more pain and misery, not less. God wants us to know that He is sovereign and that He provides and that He keeps His promises.

I am sure that Abraham and Sarah felt their anxiety begin to go away. Abraham was going to have a child. But it was not long before their plan began to backfire on them. We read in Genesis 16:4-5,

> But when Hagar knew she was pregnant, she began to treat her mistress, Sarai, with contempt. Then Sarai said to Abram, "This is all your fault! I put my servant into your arms, but now that she's pregnant she treats me with contempt. The LORD will show who's wrong-you or me!"

Aside from the clear implication given in Genesis 2:23-24, it is not until New Testament authors wrote that it would be explicitly spelled out that God intended a man to only have one wife, but you see this implied in the lives of every married man in the Old Testament. When men start taking multiple wives, trouble is never far behind!

Hagar became prideful and arrogant because she would be the mother of Abraham's child, and that as the only child, her child would inherit all Abraham's wealth. As a result Sarah became jealous that she was not going to be the mother of his descendants. Sarah then blames the whole mess on Abraham!

In Genesis 17:15-16, thirteen years after the birth of Ishmael, when Abraham was ninety-nine years old, God spoke again to Abraham and reaffirmed that He was going to make good on His promise that Abraham and Sarah would have a son of their own.

> Then God said to Abraham, "Regarding Sarai, your wife-her name will no longer be Sarai. From now on her name will be Sarah. And I will bless her and give you a son from her! Yes, I will bless her richly, and she will become the mother of many nations. Kings of nations will be among her descendants."

Abraham is stunned. How could this be possible? If he was thinking things were impossible with himself and Sarah when he was 86 they surely were impossible when he was 99! In 17:17-18 we read,

> Then Abraham bowed down to the ground, but he laughed to himself in disbelief. "How could I become a father at the age of 100?" he thought. "And how can Sarah have a baby when she is ninety years old?" So Abraham said to God, "May Ishmael live under your special blessing!"

He simply did not believe that God could do what He was promising. He was too old. Sarah was too old. But in the next verse God assures Abraham that this is exactly what He is going to do.

> No Sarah, your wife, will give birth to a son for you. You will name him Isaac, and I will confirm my covenant with him and his descendants as an everlasting covenant.

Soon after this in Genesis 18:12, Abraham was visited by the Lord again and again told Him that Abraham would have a son by Sarah who would be his heir. Sarah overheard this conversation. She outright laughed at the thought.

> So she laughed silently to herself and said, "How could a worn-out woman like me enjoy such pleasure, especially when my master—my husband—is also so old?"

Sarah laughed to herself because she did not want to disrespect Abraham's visitor (she did not know he was a messenger of God's). But God hears even silent laughter.

> Then the LORD said to Abraham, "Why did Sarah laugh? Why did she say, 'Can an old woman like me have a baby?' Is anything too hard for the LORD? I will return about this time next year, and Sarah will have a son." Sarah was afraid, so she denied it, saying, "I didn't laugh." But the LORD said, "No, you did laugh (Genesis 18:13-15).

God knows when we doubt His promises. God knows when we say to ourselves, "God will never come through for me." When we find ourselves anxious about the future we often join Sarah in laughing at God's promises to bless and provide for us. "Where's the blessing, where is the happiness, where is the joy," we laugh to ourselves, "I've been waiting for weeks, months, even years for God to come through for me, and He hasn't yet!" We all have had thoughts like this.

When we are thinking like this we need to remember God's response to Sarah, "Is anything too hard for the Lord?" His answer was to remind Sarah of His sovereignty. He waited as long as He did because He wanted Abraham and Sarah to know—beyond a shadow of a doubt—that their child was not the result of their best efforts, but was the result of God's sovereign power and faithfulness to His promise to Abraham.

God rarely does things the way we would do them or in the time frame we would do them. So if we are going to be free of anxiety about what the future holds we need to trust in the One who holds the future.

If you have ever had surgery you have a good picture of what I mean. You have to completely trust in the wisdom and intent of the physician doing the surgery. You are going to be asleep. You will have no way to personally check what is being done. If you don't trust the doctor, you won't go through with it no matter how necessary the surgery might be. You will keep looking for a doctor that you trust has the knowledge and experience in order to do the job.

God is the Great Physician. He has promised to be good to us. The question is do we trust Him? When we don't have all the answers we would like, because of God's sovereign faithfulness we can say with confidence, "I can rest in not knowing because I know He knows."

Psalm 9:10 says "Those who know your name will trust in you, for you, LORD, have never forsaken those who seek you." Ironically, the way God wants us to counter anxiety about the future is to remember what He has done in the past. It is no mistake that one of God's commands to the Israelites during the first Passover before He brought them out of Egypt was Exodus 13:8-9, "On the seventh day you must explain to your children, 'I am celebrating what the LORD did for me when I left Egypt.' This annual festival will be a visible sign to you, like a mark branded on your hand or your forehead. Let it remind you always to recite this teaching of the LORD: 'With a strong hand, the LORD rescued you from Egypt.'" He wants us to be learning that the best way to build faith and trust in His promises for the future is to keep fresh in mind His faithfulness in keeping those promises in the past.

In trying to keep this command myself, I wear a ring that says "remember me" in Hebrew. That is the main point of Deuteronomy chapter 8. "Don't forget who brought you here. Don't forget who gave you all that you have and the ability to have more. Don't forget what I have done for you. Remember Me." Whenever I see that ring, I remember. Having that reminder on my hand every day has gone a long way in helping me walk away from the trap of anxiety.

Remembering what God has done creates the foundation for a defense against anxiety. The next step is in remembering God's promises to take care of you. Promises like Isaiah 35:4 (ESV),

> Say to those who have an anxious heart, "Be strong; fear not! Behold, your God will come with vengeance, with the recompense of God. He will come and save you."

And Philippians 4:6-7,

> Do not be anxious about anything, but in everything, by prayer and petition, with thanksgiving, present your requests to God. And the peace of God, which transcends all understanding, will guard your hearts and your minds in Christ Jesus.

And 1 Peter 5:7 (NIV), "Cast all your anxiety on Him, because He cares for you."

Let me close this chapter by sharing with you the wisdom of Charles Spurgeon.

> In seasons of severe trial, the Christian has nothing on earth that he can trust to, and is therefore compelled to cast himself on his God alone. When

42

his vessel is on its beam-ends, and no human deliverance can avail, he must simply and entirely trust himself to the providence and care of God. Happy storm that wrecks a man on such a rock as this! O blessed hurricane that drives the soul to God and God alone! There is no getting at our God sometimes because of the multitude of our friends; but when a man is so poor, so friendless, so helpless that he has nowhere else to turn, he flies into his Father's arms, and is blessedly clasped therein! When he is burdened with troubles so pressing and so peculiar, that he cannot tell them to any but his God, he may be thankful for them; for he will learn more of his Lord then than at any other time. Oh, tempest-tossed believer, it is a happy trouble that drives thee to thy Father! Now that thou hast only thy God to trust to, see that thou puttest thy full confidence in him. Dishonor not thy Lord and Master by unworthy doubts and fears; but be strong in faith, giving glory to God. Show the world that thy God is worth ten thousand worlds to thee. Show rich men how rich thou art in thy poverty when the Lord God is thy helper. Show the strong man how strong thou art in thy weakness when underneath thee are the everlasting arms. Now is the time for feats of faith and valiant exploits. Be strong and very courageous, and the Lord thy God shall certainly, as surely as he built the heavens and the earth, glorify himself in thy weakness, and magnify his might in the midst of thy distress. The grandeur of the arch of heaven would be spoiled if the sky were supported by a single visible column, and your faith would lose its glory if it rested on anything discernible by the carnal eye.

FREEDOM UNDER SOVEREIGNTY MEANS

The most often given command in the Bible is "do not be afraid."

Anxiety comes from a false expectation that we should be in control.

You don't need to be anxious because God cares for you. You are important to Him.

God is not interested in making you feel capable. He is interested in helping you see and trust that He is capable.

When we don't have all the answers we want we can still say with confidence, "I can rest in not knowing because I know He knows."

VERSE TO REMEMBER

Yes, ask me for anything in my name, and I will do it!
John 14:14

LEARNING TO LIVE UNDER SOVEREIGNTY

1. What does Matthew 6:25-34 say about being anxious? What about this passage is the most helpful to you? What is the most challenging to you?
2. How did Abraham deal with anxiety over how kings would treat him because his wife Sarah was so beautiful? Was this a good response to his anxiety?
3. How did Abraham and Sarah deal with their anxiety because of God's promise that they would have a son for an heir? Did their decision help them or cause more anxiety?
4. Read 1 Peter 5:6-7. How can working at being humble help us overcome anxiety?
5. Have you ever experienced anxiety over God's timing of answering your prayers or meeting a need? How did you deal with your anxiety? Looking back would you do

    things differently now?

6.   One of the best ways to counter anxiety is to remember what God has done for you in the past. What are some things that God has done for you that you would like to remember when you are feeling anxious? Write them down.

7.   What are the things that trigger anxiety for you? What do you need to do to give God control over these areas of your life?

8.   Philippians 4:6-7 says instead of being anxious about everything we should present our requests to God in prayer. Do you take the time to present your requests to God each day? Do you feel that there are some things you can't bring to God in prayer? What are they and why do you believe you cannot give them to God?

9.   What do you think Charles Spurgeon means by saying, "Happy storm that wrecks a man on such a rock as this! O blessed hurricane that drives the soul to God and God alone?"

10.   Who do you know that struggles with anxiety that you might be able to help or pray for? Write their names down and commit to talking to them this week.

CULTIVATING FREEDOM UNDER SOVEREIGNTY

The way to counter anxiety is to boost your feelings of security. When you are feeling secure it will be very difficult to have a problem with anxiety. How might you address becoming more spiritually secure where you are? What can you do in your own life or for the people you lead to cultivate an atmosphere where feelings of security can grow?

I shared in this chapter that I wear a ring that says "Remember Me" to remind me that God is with me and in control of my life. What visible reminder of God's faithful presence could you wear or display in a prominent place where you spend a lot of time?

When people come to me for help with anxiety or worry I set up a meeting between them and a woman in my church who has really the gift of resting in God's peace. Who do you know that you could talk to or send someone to who could mentor a person who is struggling with anxiety?

C h a p t e r   3

FREEDOM TO HOPE

May the God of hope fill you with all joy and peace in believing, so that by the power of the Holy Spirit you may abound in hope.

ROMANS 15:13 (ESV)

O child of suffering, be thou patient; God has not passed thee over in his providence. He who is the feeder of sparrows, will also furnish you with what you need. Sit not down in despair; hope on, hope ever. Take up the arms of faith against a sea of trouble, and your opposition shall yet end your distresses. There is One who careth for you. His eye is fixed on you, his heart beats with pity for your woe, and his hand omnipotent shall yet bring you the needed help.

We can relax about the future and have hope no matter where we are at or what our present circumstances are. God is in control of the future and so we can have confident hope that God's promises will be kept.

C.H. SPURGEON, *MORNING AND EVENING*,
MORNING JANUARY 6

If you were to make a list of all the things you needed to live, what you believe is absolutely essential for survival, what would you put on it? Shelter? Food? Clothing? Money?

Family and friends? Medical care? What would you add to the list? Take a minute to think about that. What things would your list consist of?

Did your list include hope as something you absolutely needed to survive? You can go through most anything if you have hope. But if you lose hope, if you become hopeless, your life is over. Hope is as necessary to life as breathing. Hope is not just important. Hope is essential.

One of hardest things to see is a person who has no hope. To be hopeless is one of the scariest things in the world. I would rather be blind, I would rather be a quadriplegic, I would rather never be able to speak again than to be hopeless. Hope is essential.

The saying goes "home is where the heart is." It is just as true to say "hope is where the heart is." What do you put your hope in?

You have heard that popular proverb, "Hope springs eternal in the human breast." That is not true, is it? Sometimes hope dies. When hope dies, marriages die, relationships end, families are torn apart, addictions rise up to take their place, jobs are lost, businesses fold, dreams die, and sometimes hopelessness even claims the very life of the person who lost hope.

Life has no shortage of problems. If life were not so full of disappointments, struggles, pain, loss, and challenges, perhaps hope would not be so important to have. But there is no shortage of those things, is there?

Storms come into our lives that are as devastating to us as hurricane Katrina was to the people of New Orleans. There are people in my congregation as I am writing this that are going through major life-storms. One is dealing with the loss of a son to an automobile accident. Others are dealing with children who are addicted to drugs. Others are dealing with the pain of divorce. Others are dealing with friends who are struggling with thoughts of suicide. Another is struggling with the pain of a friend who shot himself. While writing this chapter, I conducted a funeral service for a man who lost his wife of 48 years to a cancer. He has no family. They have all died. He is alone. He struggles with hopelessness.

You might be struggling in similar storms yourselves. You might be in a storm of financial trouble. You might be wondering how the mortgage is going to get paid this month. You might be even wondering where your next meal is coming from. Perhaps you are now wondering what is next or how life is going to be after the storm.

What do you put your hope in? People? Money? Influence? Fame? Luck? I want to share with you a passage from the Bible that talks about the place where we should be placing our hope, Psalm 146.

> Don't put your confidence in powerful people; there is no help for you there. When they breathe their last, they return to the earth, and all their plans die with them. But joyful are those who have the God of Israel as their helper, whose hope is in the LORD their God. He made heaven and earth, the sea, and everything in them. He keeps every promise forever.

One of the greatest gifts of grace that you have when you trust in Christ is the assurance of hope. The reason God sent Jesus to this earth to live and die and rise again was so that you could claim the hope in this Psalm for yourself. Jesus came to give you hope. He came to free you from hopes that don't live up to the hype so you could be set free to live and run and dream with a hope that cannot be stolen, that cannot be broken, that cannot be lost, and that cannot fail.

God is a God who keeps all His promises. When God makes a promise He keeps it. No one who hopes in the Lord will ever be put to shame, because He keeps all His promises. He doesn't renege on His word, no power can stop Him. He doesn't need anyone's permission to go ahead with His plans. Every promise God makes He keeps. When your heart is in Him and your hope is in Him, you have an unshakable foundation for hope. Romans 8 makes this abundantly clear,

> If God is for us, who can ever be against us?... I am convinced that nothing can ever separate us from his love. Death can't, and life can't. The angels can't, and the demons can't. Our fears for today, our worries about tomorrow, and even the powers of hell can't keep God's love away. Whether we are high above the sky or in the deepest ocean, nothing in all creation will ever be able to separate us from the love of God that is revealed in Christ Jesus our Lord.

HOW DO YOU KNOW THIS IS TRUE?

The foundation of your hope is in the cross of Christ. Why is that? Because there is no greater thing that God could do to prove the length and depth of His love and His commitment to His promises to those who trust Him than that. Paul says in Romans 8:32, "Since He did not spare even his own Son but gave him up for us all, won't he also give us everything else?"

God wants you to know, "You can put your hope in Me because I have not held back anything from you and have committed all that I am to insure that what I promise will come to pass. Nothing is greater than Myself and that is what I have given you through the work of Jesus Christ. You have the righteousness of Christ given in place of your guilt, and you have Him as your Brother praying and advocating for you before Me. You have My Spirit living and moving in you connecting you to Me at all times, and interceding for you every minute of the day. And you have my promises to love you, to provide for you, to rescue you, to comfort you, to uphold you, to guide you, to strengthen you, and carry you home to Me without fail. All I have and all that I Am is yours because you are Mine, and I never forsake My own."

One of the most powerful expressions of this hope is Psalm 23:4, "Even though I walk through the valley of the shadow of death, I will fear no evil, for you are with me." What a beautiful expression of hope! No matter how dark things get, no matter what storm comes, no matter how heavy life becomes, we will fear no evil, because we know He is with us.

We can be confident in our hope in the love and grace and salvation of God because God always wins. His will always prevails. He never loses one of His own. Jesus says, "No one can snatch them away from me, for my Father has given them to me, and he is more powerful than anyone else. No one can snatch them from the Father's hand. The Father and I are one" (John 10:28-30).

Faith in Christ comes with this hope.

There is no pre-qualification of goodness or success to be given this hope. It does not matter at all whether you are homeless or living in a mansion. None of that matters. Hebrews 11:1 says, "Faith is the confidence that what we hope for will actually happen; it gives us assurance about things we cannot see." One comes with the other. Faith and hope are two sides of the same coin. To have faith is to have hope. To have hope, you must have faith. If you take away one you cannot have the other. When you place your hope in God by accepting the grace and forgiveness He offers through Jesus Christ, your feet are brought to stand firmly on the hope that God promises.

What do you put your hope in? If you want the rock-solid hope that God offers, you have to have faith in Him. Hope is where the heart is. To build your hope in Him, you need to build your faith in God. That happens in two ways.

STUDY

My friend Charlie Jones was famous for saying, "You'll be the same person you are today in five years except for two things: the people you meet and the books you read...and considering who you are now, you better get reading!" That is so true! The Bible is a big book of all the promises God has made to those who trust Him. It is very difficult to know what those promises are unless you take the time to read them! You can begin to rid yourself of a lot of unnecessary depression, guilt, anxiety, fear, and shame just by becoming aware of all the promises God has made to you. Not only that, but reading the Bible will show you that God not only makes great promises, but that He is the kind of God who keeps His promises. When you read the Bible you will see the kind of person God is; that He is faithful to the great and the small, the powerful and the powerless, to the young and to the old. He is faithful to keep His promises even when His people stumble and fall.

You need to read. If you don't like reading, listen to someone else read the Bible to you. Have your wife or husband read it to you. You can get the Bible on tape, CD, MP3, and DVD. There is no excuse for not getting into the

Word! The starting point for building your hope in God is by reading the Bible so that you know the God whom your hope is in and the promises He has made to you.

PRACTICE

Reading and studying the Bible is preparation. When you close your Bible and walk out the door, practice starts. You control what you put into your head. God controls what goes into your life. Things are going to happen that are going to give you opportunity to learn to lean on the God of those promises.

The foundation for an unshakable hope is sure, but faith and trust to lean on that foundation in hope is something you learn to do as you walk with God through your life. In that sense, you don't just get hope, hope is grown. You strengthen hope by being in places with God where your hope in Him is pushed and stretched. Romans 5:3-5 (ESV) says, "More than that, we rejoice in our sufferings, knowing that suffering produces endurance, and endurance produces character, and character produces hope, and hope does not put us to shame, because God's love has been poured into our hearts through the Holy Spirit who has been given to us."

When you read the Bible, you read about how God came through for others. When you live in the hope of Christ you experience God coming through on those promises for you.

HOPE IS WHERE THE HEART IS.

Many people put their hope in money, or possessions, or success, or people. Every once in a while I hear someone say something like, "I'm waiting for my ship to come in." But most of those people have never sent any ships out other than an occasional lottery ticket.

Albert Einstein is famous for saying, "The height of insanity is doing the same thing and expecting a different result." We are told, taught, and even bullied into thinking that hope is something we can buy, build, or own. Why do we continue to act as if this is true? If you are going to believe that you might as well believe the world is flat! The hope that money, success, and possessions brings is weak and short lived. It fails more often than it succeeds. That is our experience. Yet we keep thinking this time it will be different.

This reminds me of an illustration Jesus used at the end of the Sermon on the Mount in Matthew 7:24-27 (NIV),

> Anyone who listens to my teaching and follows it is wise, like a person who builds a house on solid rock. Though the rain comes in torrents and the floodwaters rise and the winds beat against that house, it won't collapse because it is built on bedrock.

> But anyone who hears my teaching and ignores it is foolish, like a person who builds a house on sand. When the rains and floods come and the winds beat against that house, it will collapse with a mighty crash.

When we put our hope in things like money, or possessions, or success, we are like the man who built his house on the sand. But joyful are those who have the God of Israel as their helper, whose hope is in the LORD their God. He made heaven and earth, the sea, and everything in them. He keeps every promise forever.

FREEDOM UNDER SOVEREIGNTY MEANS

God is the "God of hope" because He is the source of hope. He is the God of hope because any promise He makes he can keep.

Jesus came to free you to have a hope that cannot be stolen, that cannot be broken, that cannot be lost, and that cannot fail.

We can be confident in our hope of the love and grace and salvation of God because God always wins. His will always prevails.

When you place your hope in God by accepting the grace and forgiveness He offers through Jesus Christ, your feet are brought to stand firmly on the hope that God promises.

You can begin to rid yourself of a lot of unnecessary depression, guilt, anxiety, fear, and shame just by becoming aware of all the promises God has made to you and placing your trust in the God who made those promises.

When you read the Bible, you read about how God came through for others. When you live in the hope of Christ you experience God coming through on those promises for you.

VERSE TO REMEMBER

May the God of hope fill you with all joy and peace in believing, so that by the power of the Holy Spirit you may abound in hope.
Romans 15:13 (ESV)

LEARNING TO LIVE UNDER SOVEREIGNTY

1. Read through Psalm 146. What does this Psalm teach us about where we should put our hope?
2. What promises are given by God in this Psalm?
3. Read Matthew 7:24-27. What does this passage teach about where we should build our hope and why?

4.   What are some examples of building hope on the sand? What do you think attracts people to place their hope in those things?

5.   How does the sovereignty of God ensure that He is a safe and solid place on which to build our hope?

6.   What do you make regular time to read, listen to, and watch? Are the things you listed helpful to building your hope in God's promises?

7.   Are you facing any challenges in your life right now that would benefit from having a stronger and clearer hope in God and His promises to you? Write them down.

8.   Look at your answers for question 2. Can any of these promises help you with the challenges you wrote down for question 7?

9.   What are some ways in which God has come through for you in your life?

10. Do you have a way to remember the prayers God has answered for you and how He has provided for you in the past? If so, share that idea with someone who might benefit from your help in increasing their hope. If not, what might you be able to commit to this week so that you can have a running record of the ways that God has come through for you?

CULTIVATING FREEDOM UNDER SOVEREIGNTY

My friend Charlie Jones said, "You'll be the same person you are today in five years except for two things: the people you meet and the books you read...and considering who you are now, you better get reading!" What we read, watch, and listen to has a profound effect on our hope.

I recently talked with a high school student who was struggling with hopelessness. I discovered through talking to him that he was spending hours and hours a day listening to music that was expressing the hopelessness of the people who were singing! No wonder he was so depressed! I made him a CD of Christian Rock music that I knew he would like and had him listen to that. He was very grateful and did that. His struggle with hopelessness faded significantly within one week. What are some other ideas you might give to a person who is feeling hopeless?

Make time to read your Bible every day and encourage the members of your family or congregation to do the same.

Each chapter of this book has a memory verse that points to a promise that God has made to all of His children. Take the time to memorize them. Copy them down in your favorite translation and leave them on the bathroom mirror or on the steering wheel of your car so that you see them all the time until you memorize them.

Chapter 4

REST FROM DEPRESSION

Though a thousand fall at your side, though ten thousand are dying around you, these evils will not touch you. Just open your eyes, and see how the wicked are punished. If you make the LORD your refuge, if you make the Most High your shelter, no evil will conquer you; no plague will come near your home. For he will order his angels to protect you wherever you go. They will hold you up with their hands so you won't even hurt your foot on a stone.

PSALM 91:7-12

Deep depression of spirit is the most grievous of all trials; all besides is as nothing. Well might the suffering Savior cry to his God, "Be not far from me," for above all other seasons a man needs his God when his heart is melted within him because of heaviness. Believer, come near the cross this morning, and humbly adore the King of glory as having once been brought far lower, in mental distress and inward anguish, than any one among us; and mark his fitness to become a faithful High Priest, who can be touched with a feeling of our infirmities.

C.H. SPURGEON, *MORNING AND EVENING*,
MORNING APRIL 12

LUTHER'S BAD YEAR

April 22, 1527, was yet another bad day in a year-long-string of bad days for Martin Luther. A dizzy spell forced him to stop preaching in the middle of his sermon. Ten years had gone by since publishing his *95 Theses* against the abuse of indulgences. Luther had been buffeted by political and theological storms as a result of that publication and at times his life had been in danger. Now he was battling other reformers over the meaning of the Lord's Supper. To Luther, their errors were as great as those of Rome—the very gospel was at stake—and Luther was deeply disturbed and angry. He suffered severe depression.

Several months later on July 6, as friends arrived for dinner, Luther felt an intense buzzing in his left ear. He went to lie down, when suddenly he called, "Water or I'll die!" He became cold, and he was convinced he had seen his last night. In a loud prayer, he surrendered himself to God's will.

With a doctor's help, Luther partially regained his strength. But this depression and illness overcame him again in August, September, and again in late December. Looking back on one of his bouts, he wrote his friend Melanchthon, "I spent more than a week in death and hell. My entire body was in pain, and I still tremble. Completely abandoned by Christ, I labored under the vacillations and storms of desperation and blasphemy against God. But through the prayers of the saints [his friends], God began to have mercy on me and pulled my soul from the inferno below."

Meanwhile, in August, the plague had erupted in Wittenberg. As fear spread, so did many of the townspeople. But Luther considered it his duty to remain and care for the sick. Even though his wife was pregnant, Luther's house was transformed into a hospital, and he ended up watching many of his friends die. Then his son became ill. Not until late November did the epidemic abate....[2]

Talk about a bad year!

My friend, have you ever struggled with depression? I have. I dare say we all have. All of us have bad things happen to us. Like the Great Reformer, all of us find ourselves in situations where we wake up and just feel depressed; times when nothing seems to go right, times when nothing we do seems to be working, times when the problems just keep piling up and nothing ever seems to get resolved.

As I am writing this chapter, many of the people in my church are right now in the midst of or are just entering into a season of difficulty. There are people in our church family who have just recently lost a father, another who has been diagnosed with cancer, another had a teenage friend cut themselves, and yet another is struggling through the pain of divorce. In the past month I have counseled a friend whose 40 year marriage is breaking apart, performed six funerals, been on the phone into the early morning hours with a man who was in tears struggling with depression, and I had to put down my dog. It is in times like these that we need to hold tight to God's goodness. One person came up to me recently and declared they must have kicked God's dog because God wasn't doing them any favors. Have you ever felt like that?

When you are depressed, you lose your energy. You lose your drive, your focus, your productivity. Not only that, but you end up losing your spiritual strength as well. You find it harder to pray, and perhaps you stop praying all together. God seems further and further away, until you come to the conclusion that God is not for us but against us... if He even cares at all.

HABAKKUK'S BAD YEAR

Martin Luther was not the first person to feel depressed and abandoned by God. Habakkuk, the author the Old Testament book that bears his name, was feeling depressed as he sat down to pray and write his short three chapter book. He lived in the darkest days that Jerusalem had lived to see. He was a prophet who lived in the final days of Judah just before the world power of Babylon would raze Jerusalem to the ground and carry the inhabitants of his beloved city off into exile in 587BC.

The people of Judah had long abandoned God for the "so-called gods" of other nations. The leadership was corrupt. The king, Jehoiakim (like so many kings before him), paid no attention to the prophets God sent to warn him of the consequences for leading God's people astray.

Habakkuk was discouraged, frustrated, and he was losing hope. He looked around at his beloved city of Jerusalem and saw nothing good. God was not helping things and was not giving any sign that things were going to get better any time soon.

Thankfully for us, Habakkuk was not yet so depressed that he had stopped praying.

The book of Habakkuk is really a prayer journal that God directed him to make public in which he recorded two of his prayers to God, God's responses to those prayers, and his final response of praise to God in light of His answers. In it we find a potent spiritual treatment for depression. In the final chapter of Habakkuk he writes,

> LORD, I have heard of your fame; I stand in awe of your deeds, O LORD. Renew them in our day, in our time make them known; in wrath remember mercy. God came from Teman, the Holy One from

Chapter 4: Rest from Depression

Mount Paran.

His glory covered the heavens and his praise filled the earth. His splendor was like the sunrise; rays flashed from his hand, where his power was hidden. Plague went before him; pestilence followed his steps. He stood, and shook the earth; he looked, and made the nations tremble. The ancient mountains crumbled and the age-old hills collapsed. His ways are eternal. I saw the tents of Cushan in distress, the dwellings of Midian in anguish. Were you angry with the rivers, O LORD? Was your wrath against the streams? Did you rage against the sea when you rode with your horses and your victorious chariots? You uncovered your bow, you called for many arrows.

You split the earth with rivers; the mountains saw you and writhed. Torrents of water swept by; the deep roared and lifted its waves on high. Sun and moon stood still in the heavens at the glint of your flying arrows, at the lightning of your flashing spear. In wrath you strode through the earth and in anger you threshed the nations. You came out to deliver your people, to save your anointed one. You crushed the leader of the land of wickedness, you stripped him from head to foot.

With his own spear you pierced his head when his warriors stormed out to scatter us, gloating as though about to devour the wretched who were in hiding. You trampled the sea with your horses, churning the great waters. I heard my heart pounded, my lips quivered at the sound; decay crept into my bones, and my legs trembled. Yet I will wait patiently for the day of calamity to come on the nation invading us.

Though the fig tree does not bud and there are no grapes on the vines, though the olive crop fails and the fields produce no food, though there are no sheep in the pen and no cattle in the stalls, yet I will rejoice in the LORD, I will be joyful in God my Savior. The Sovereign LORD is my strength; he makes my feet like the feet of a deer, he enables me to go on the heights.

The key to fighting depression that Habakkuk reveals to us in this chapter lies in resting in the sovereign goodness of God.

It is not enough to admit that we are helpless. It is not enough to acknowledge that we are not up to the task, as important as that is. We need to bring ourselves to rest in the promise that God is good and that He is committed to the good of His people.

GOD IS GOOD

God's goodness is the cornerstone of why He is worthy of our heartfelt praise and obedience. The greatness of God lies very much in the goodness of God. Psalm 145:6-9 says,

Your awe-inspiring deeds will be on every tongue; I will proclaim your greatness. Everyone will share the story of your wonderful goodness; they will sing with joy about your righteousness. The LORD is merciful and compassionate, slow to get angry and filled with unfailing love. The LORD is good to everyone.

The Lord is good to everyone. God is never

underhanded. He is never deceitful. He is never unjust. He always does what is best. He always keeps His promises. He always judges with righteousness. No one can justly accuse Him of wrong.

There is a biblical reality that we need to understand about God's goodness and I'm going to give it to you straight up. The good that God has for you is often given in and discovered after times of distress and pain. Have you noticed that? That is God's *modus operandi*! When God wants to do you good, it very often first appears to us dressed as pain, challenge, distress, or trouble.

God's goodness drives Him to do what it takes to give you His best and grow you and transform you into His best. God's goodness does not drive Him to leave you comfortable and happy all the time. To get God's best we need to change and change is painful. This is the case all through the Bible. Abraham had to be willing to put his only son on the altar. Joseph had to be sold as a slave. Moses had to hide in the desert for 40 years. Job had to lose his possessions, his family, and his health. David had to run from Saul, and then from his own son Absalom. Jonah had to be swallowed by a whale.

When Paul was converted, God announced in Acts 9:15 "Paul is my chosen instrument to take my message to the Gentiles and to kings, as well as to the people of Israel." Paul was God's chosen instrument. Is that not what we all want to be? It is our dream to be the chosen instrument of God. But we need to remember that verse 15 is not the end of God's pronouncement. He concludes in verse 16, "And I will show him *how much he must suffer* for my name's sake" (emphasis mine).

We often have the truncated idea that suffering is merely *corrective*. But suffering can also be *constructive*. Suffering is often a sign of God's good pleasure with us. Remember the words of James who wrote in James 1:2-4,

> Dear brothers and sisters, when troubles come your way, consider it an opportunity for great joy. For you know that when your faith is tested, your endurance has a chance to grow. So let it grow, for when your endurance is fully developed, you will be perfect and complete, needing nothing.

The key to overcoming depression is resting in trusting that God is good, *not* in understanding everything that God does or why. You cannot expect to understand how God intends to bring about good in every situation. He is *God*. If we could understand everything about why He does things the way He does them He wouldn't be much of a God. His thinking is above our thinking. His ways are above our ways. But His ways are always good.

One of the problems of modern Evangelicalism is its seemingly confined focus on the safe, kind, and friendly characteristics of God. For instance we are fine with Habakkuk's description of God in 3:3-4: "His brilliant splendor fills the heavens, and the earth is filled with his praise. His coming is as brilliant as the sunrise. Rays of light flash from his hands, where his awesome power is hidden."

That is the God we "know and love" in our American evangelical culture. But when we get to verse 5 we start to get uncomfortable really fast. "Pestilence marches before him; plague follows close behind. When he stops, the earth shakes. When he looks, the nations tremble. He shatters the everlasting mountains and levels the eternal hills."

"Pestilence marches before him; plague follows close behind." This doesn't sound like the same "loving" God we hear about in most churches or about in books by Christian authors. In the face of war, rape, murder, racism, and corporate corruption (all of which were going on in Habakkuk's day), we are tempted to doubt the sovereign goodness of God. Why would a sovereign good God allow so much pain, suffering, and evil? This in fact was one of the central complaints in Habakkuk's prayers. He says in 1:13, "But you are pure and cannot stand the sight of evil. Will you wink at their treachery? Should you be silent while the wicked swallow up people more righteous than they?"

God's answer is not what we would expect. He does not give easy answers. He does not give a formula that Habakkuk can use to decipher the good that God intends by allowing bad things to happen. If He had, there would not be any reason for my writing this book! God simply asserts His sovereignty and control over all that happens in His world and declares that in the end good will triumph and all evil will be judged and punished. This side of heaven we will not have all the answers. That is the reality of living by faith and not by sight. We need to take God at His word, "For I know the plans I have for you," says the LORD. "They are plans for good and not for disaster, to give you a future and a hope" (Jeremiah 29:11).

If you are trapped by depression, let me give you four directives to help you to get free.

DON'T STOP PRAYING

The goal of the devil and the temptation of your soul is to attack your connection to and conversation with God. You cannot break your relationship with Christ, but you *can* close your eyes to it. You *can* forget about it. You *can* doubt it. Don't give in to that temptation. Pray!

If you cannot bring yourself to pray, then thank God that Jesus is always praying and interceding for you before your

Father. It is a great comfort to know that when the devil was going after Peter, Jesus was interceding for him, even though Peter was not aware of what Satan was doing. Jesus told him in Luke 22:31-32, "Simon, Simon, Satan has asked to sift each of you like wheat. But I have pleaded in prayer for you, Simon, that your faith should not fail." Reader, Jesus prays for you in just the same way. Remember Hebrews 7:24-25, "But because Jesus lives forever, his priesthood lasts forever. Therefore he is able, once and forever, to save those who come to God through him. *He lives forever to intercede with God on their behalf*" (emphasis mine).

Thank God that the Holy Spirit is always praying for you with groanings that cannot be put into words. Remember what God promises in Romans 8:26-27,

> And the Holy Spirit helps us in our weakness. For example, we don't know what God wants us to pray for. But the Holy Spirit prays for us with groanings that cannot be expressed in words. And the Father who knows all hearts knows what the Spirit is saying, for the Spirit pleads for us believers in harmony with God's own will.

No matter how bad or dark things get, do not under any circumstances stop praying. Do not stop reading God's Word. Do not distance yourself from your church family. In times like that you need those supports more, not less.

UNDERSTAND THAT GOD IS TEACHING YOU TO REST IN HIM

We trust in so many things to save and protect us. We trust in our abilities and talents. We trust in our money. We trust in our networks and contacts. We trust in our possessions.

God wants you to know that the only possession you need is Christ. The only Person you can count on without fail is Jesus. The only power worth anything is the power of the Holy Spirit. And the only true place to rest is in the hollow of the hand of God the Father Almighty.

That is what He is teaching you when you are going through those times. That is where He is leading you. This is not something you ever finish learning in this life. He will keep taking you deeper and deeper until He brings you home.

USE DISCERNMENT IN THESE TIMES OF HARD TRIAL

When God brings seasons of pain and suffering and limitation into your life, you need to honestly ask yourself this question: "Is God cleaning me or growing me?" Is there some real habitual sin you are allowing to go unchecked in your life that God wants you to acknowledge and repent of? If the answer is yes, then own up to it. Ask for forgiveness and do whatever you need to do to give it up.

If the answer is honestly no, then understand that God wants to grow you. Ask God to help you to trust that He knows what is best and to make it clear what he wants you to learn about God and about yourself.

REMEMBER GOD'S PAST GRACE

The past gives hope for the future. Habakkuk's hope for the future was grounded in the flawless track record of God's salvation of Israel in the past. I love the New Living Translation's translation of Habakkuk 3:2, "I have heard all about you, LORD. I am filled with awe by your amazing works. In this time of our deep need, help us again as you did in years gone by." When we remember God's past grace, we begin to build up hope in God's promise of future grace.

WHAT GOD CAN DO WITH A BAD YEAR

Let's return to Martin Luther. During that horrific year of 1527, Luther took time to remember the tenth anniversary of his publication against indulgences, noting the deeper meaning of his trials: "The only comfort against raging Satan is that we have God's Word to save the souls of believers." Sometime that year, Luther expanded that thought into the hymn he is most famous for: "A Mighty Fortress Is Our God."

> And though this world with devils filled should threaten to undo us
> We will not fear, for God has willed his truth to triumph through us.
> The prince of darkness grim? We tremble not for him.
> His rage we can endure, for lo! his doom is sure.
> One little Word shall fell him.

For 479 years, that hymn has been sung in churches around the world. It is right up there with *Amazing Grace* as one of best loved and best known hymns of all time. God's sovereign goodness shines like the sun in that song. God used that horrible year with all its pain and suffering and loss and produced this diamond that we treasure to this day.

Don't ever doubt God's goodness. Don't ever think that the darkness of depression cannot be banished in an instant in the light of His goodness. For God knows the plans He has for you. Plans for good and not disaster. Plans for a hope and a future.

FREEDOM UNDER SOVEREIGNTY MEANS

It is not enough to admit that we are helpless. It is not enough to acknowledge that we are not up to the task, as important as that is. We need to bring ourselves to rest in the promise that God is good and that He is committed to the good of His people.

The key to overcoming depression is resting in God's goodness, *not* in understanding everything that God does or why He does it.

No matter how bad or dark things get, do not under any circumstances stop praying.

God wants you to know that the only possession you need is Christ.

When God brings seasons of pain and suffering and limitation into your life you need to honestly ask yourself this question: "Is God cleaning me or growing me?"

When we remember God's past grace, we begin to build up hope in God's promise of future grace.

VERSE TO REMEMBER

For I know the plans I have for you," says the LORD. "They are plans for good and not for disaster, to give you a future and a hope.
Jeremiah 29:11

LEARNING TO LIVE UNDER SOVEREIGNTY

1. What are some of the signs of depression?
2. How did depression effect Martin Luther? How did it effect Habakkuk?
3. What actions did Habakkuk take to deal with his depression?
4. How did God respond to Habakkuk's prayers?
5. What are some situations or things that may cause

depression?

6.   How did understanding God's sovereignty help Habakkuk deal with his depression?

7.   How can understanding God's sovereignty help you when you are struggling with depression?

8.   We are often frustrated going through difficult times because we don't understand why a good God would allow us to experience such times. What can you do to address that frustration in light of the fact that God is sovereign and good? What Bible verses might be a help in these times?

9.   Which of the four directives is the most helpful to you? Which is the most challenging?

10.   How might you be able to help someone else who is going through a time of depression?

Cultivating Freedom Under Sovereignty

When people find themselves in a season of great trial and difficulty their first response is often something like, "What did I do to deserve this?" or as a person in my church shared with me, "I must have kicked God's dog because He is not doing me any favors." We automatically assume that trouble and challenges are corrective. We do not often think that suffering can be constructive. We rarely say in times of trouble, "Wow! God must be getting ready to do something great in my life!" Helping people to see that God uses everything that comes into our lives for good is an essential truth we need to embrace about our sovereign God when we are battling depression. What are some ways you might be able to help people get into the habit of thinking that God often uses pain to bless us?

Begin a small group or set a regular time at your church where people come together just to share what is going on in their lives and bring these needs to God in group prayer. Groups that focus just on praying for each other have been a great comfort to me and my family.

Read biographies or teach about Christian leaders like Martin Luther, John Calvin, Jonathan Edwards, or Charles Spurgeon. Each of these leaders struggled with periods of depression. Seeing how they dealt with it and overcame it can give you encouragement and direction when you or people you know struggle with depression.

Chapter 5

FREEDOM TO LIVE A LIFE OF JOY

You love him even though you have never seen
him. Though you do not see him now, you trust
him; and you rejoice with a glorious, inexpressible
joy.

1 PETER 1:8

Our hearts are knit unto him: we are his members,
and though for a while we may suffer as our Head
once suffered, yet we are even now blessed with
heavenly blessings in him. We have the earnest of
our inheritance in the comforts of the Spirit, which
are neither few nor small. Inheritors of joy for ever,
we have foretastes of our portion. There are streaks
of the light of joy to herald our eternal sunrising.
Our riches are beyond the sea; our city with firm
foundations lies on the other side the river; gleams
of glory from the spirit-world cheer our hearts, and
urge us onward. Truly is it said of us, "Happy art
thou, O Israel; who is like unto thee, O people
saved by the Lord?"

C.H. SPURGEON, *MORNING AND EVENING*,
SEPTEMBER 27, MORNING

In what may well be his most influential book, *Religious
Affections*, Jonathan Edwards wrote,

That religion which God requires does not consist

74

in weak, dull, and lifeless wishes, raising us but a little above a state of indifference: God, in his word, greatly insists that we be "fervent in spirit," and that our hearts be vigorously engaged in religion.

The things of religion are so great, that our emotional response to God and His work doesn't do God or us justice unless it is lively and powerful. In nothing is emotional vigor so requisite, as in religion; and in nothing is lukewarmness so odious.

Though true grace has various degrees, and there are some that are but babes in Christ, in whom the exercise of emotions towards God is comparatively weak; yet everyone that has the power of godliness in his heart, has his heart exercised towards God and divine things, with such strength and vigor that they prevail in him above all carnal or natural affections: for every true disciple of Christ loves Him above father or mother, wife and children, brothers and sisters, even than their own life. Wherever true religion is, there are vigorous exercises of emotions towards God and His Word (Taken and edited from *Religious Affections*).

One of the affections or passions that Edwards was talking about was joy. The joy that comes because of the triumph of Christ on that first Easter Sunday. The aim of this chapter is to make joy your destination.

ROBBED OF JOY

I have it on good authority that the islands around Indonesia are among the most beautiful in the world-crystalline tropical water, beautiful reefs with fish colored in every color of the rainbow, powerful waves, and tranquil bays.

Tourists, surfers, and scuba divers from around the world have discovered these hidden jewels and pay large sums of money to enjoy this unspoiled aquatic playground.

But many of the locals won't swim. Neither will they dive, surf, wade, bathe, or do anything else that places their bodies in the warm, inviting water. Their fear of the water is so powerful that even though they are surrounded by ocean and must sail out in fishing boats for their daily sustenance, hardly any of the islanders ever learned to swim.

Why do they deny themselves the pleasure of exploring the natural wonders all around them? Because a long time ago, someone told them a lie. Someone told them that the ocean was full of demons and that swimming in it would bring harm to themselves and their families. And many Indonesian islanders still believe it.

Just as for centuries those island people have missed out on the joy of frolicking in the surf and exploring their underwater world, so there are many people today who are missing out on the joy of knowing Christ and walking in fellowship with God. They believe that God is some kind of cosmic killjoy who wants to take away their fun and make their lives dull, boring, and utterly miserable.

Too many people have come to believe that the description "joyful Christian" is just as much an oxymoron as "jumbo shrimp." Nothing could be further from the truth.

WE TALK THE TALK, BUT DON'T WALK THE WALK

Joy is one of those things that we like to talk about but don't often express in how we talk, how we act, how we work, or in how we relate to people.

Even if we know we are supposed to have joy in God, it

too often seems to evade us. The wonder and joy of the freedom we have in Christ seems to be quickly replaced with the reality that our family, work, and world is full of problems, challenges, and heartaches that don't seem to create a joy-friendly atmosphere. Joy seems evasive, short-lived. It even seems sometimes to be…well…confusing.

Yet the Bible is full of promises of joy, commands to be joyful and to rejoice, descriptions of believers as being full of joy, exhortations not to lose joy, and encouragements to keep and even to increase our joy. Take 1 Peter 1:8-9 (NIV) for instance,

> Though you have not seen him, you love him; and even though you do not see him now, you believe in him and are filled with an inexpressible and glorious joy, for you are receiving the goal of your faith, the salvation of your souls.

Our love and faith in God produces joy. Notice how this joy is described. It is an *inexpressible* joy. It is a joy that cannot be fully expressed or explained with words. All attempts to describe the breadth and depth of this joy fall utterly short of reality.

It is a *glorious* joy. Peter attempts to do as much justice as he can in describing this joy by saying that it is glorious or full of glory. That is to say, it is divine in its origin. It is produced by and is rooted in the Holy Spirit. This is a supernatural joy that comes from God and is full of His glory.

We are *filled* with this joy. The Greek literally says "you rejoice with an inexpressible and glorious joy." This joy that the Spirit reveals to us and gives to us is the cause of great and constant rejoicing for those in whom the Holy Spirit dwells. As a result Christians are always full of divine joy that comes from the Spirit of Joy who gives us life and breath.

THE GIFT OF JOY

It is an undeniable biblical fact that the Holy Spirit works to create a glorious and inexpressible joy in the life of every believer. I want you to be fully convinced of this reality.

Jesus died not only to forgive you, but to *bring you joy*. Forgiveness is fantastic. That alone is what so many saw as their reason for coming to Christ, and it is reason enough to be sure. The truth is that forgiveness is only the tip of the iceberg. The good news of the gospel is far more fantastic than simply forgiveness! Christians are not merely forgiven. You are changed! You are adopted as sons and daughters by God. You have God Almighty as your Father in the most intimate and loving sense of that word. You call Him "Abba," which you could translate into English as "Daddy." And we have been promised that when our time here is done, and our spiritual growth here in these bodies—still pulled by the curse of sin—is complete, we will join the saints that have gone before us and see our Savior, our Counselor and our Father face to face and begin a stage of life that will be more real, full, and satisfying than you or I ever thought possible.

God wants you to know three important things about this God-given joy.

IT IS PART OF THE GOAL OF YOUR FAITH

God's people are consistently described throughout the Bible as a joyous people. It is one of the identifying marks of the believer (Romans 14:17). Joy is one of the fruits of the Spirit in Galatians 5:22. In Philippians 4:4 we are commanded to rejoice. Joy is one of the clearest descriptions of the saints and angels in heaven (Revelation 19:6-7). There is no doubt that joy is one of the fruits of conversion (Acts 16:34). Hebrews 12:2 (NIV) says that "for the joy set before him endured the cross, scorning its shame." That joy that He saw was the joy of doing His Father's will: securing an inexpressible and glorious joy for every member of His adopted family. Joy is one of the goals of our salvation.

JOY IS THE FRUIT OF OUR HOPE IN CHRIST

The second thing you need to know about this joy is that this joy is the automatic response to the sure hope of our future glory with Christ. So often our joy is challenged, clouded over, and even outright attacked by the circumstances of life. Like Peter, we can become so impressed by the waves of the sea that long to drag us down to the bottom of the ocean that we forget we are walking with the Lord of Heaven and Earth.

As surely as Peter was lifted back to the surface of the water by His Master, there is nothing that can keep God's promise of salvation from being fulfilled. Whenever we feel lost, or feel down and depressed, if we refocus our thoughts on Jesus and the awesome promises He has given us and the hope that He has secured for us, that joy will begin to well back up in our souls and revive us.

You are forgiven. God loves you. His Spirit lives in you and has given you a heart for God and has marked you as His special child. Heaven is your final destination. The Sovereign Lord of the universe has promised to bring you there. That is cause for great joy and rejoicing!

THIS JOY COMES FROM BEING IN GOD'S PRESENCE

But most fully, this inexpressible and glorious joy is the

joy of being with God and enjoying Him in the same way that Jesus enjoys His Father. As fantastic as the joy of all God's promises are, as wonderful as His love for you is, what the joy of the Christian is grounded in, and rooted in, and watered by is the joy of seeing and being with God. God is the goal of your salvation. The joy of the Christian is not the promises, or the rewards, *but God Himself.* The gifts are great but they are nothing compared to the Giver.

I want to make it very clear that what I am talking about here is joy and not happiness. They are not the same. There are two very important differences between happiness and joy.

THE DIFFERENCE BETWEEN JOY AND HAPPINESS

The first is in joy's intensity. Feeling joy is a big step above feeling happy. I was happy when Charlie Jones and I finished writing the draft for our book *Finding Freedom in Forgiveness*, but I felt joy when Harvest House agreed to publish it. I felt happy when Mandi told me she was pregnant with our third child. But I felt joy when I first held little Rachel Lauren when she was born.

Joy makes your heart beat faster. It makes your head spin. It gives you goose bumps. It makes you smile from ear to ear. It physically affects you, that's why joy is called an *affection*, because it affects you physically when you feel that strong an emotion.

The second difference is that happiness is very fleeting and fickle. When things are going well, we feel happy. But when the circumstances that make us happy are gone, often, so is the happiness.

Joy is more robust, more permanent. Even when the experience or circumstances that first occasioned joy are gone, joy can still be there. 1 Peter 5:8 is an excellent example of this. "Though you have not seen him, you love him; and even though you do not see him now, you believe in him and are filled with an inexpressible and glorious joy." The people that Peter was writing to were on their own. Peter and the other apostles who founded the church were gone. They were being persecuted, ostracized, and even imprisoned. Yet in the midst of all these trials and hardships what stood out about these people was that their faith and trust in God had filled them *with an inexpressible and glorious joy.* Joy outlasts happiness. It is much more powerful. It is far more enduring than happiness.

I know what many of you are thinking. You're thinking, "I wish I knew that kind of joy." Or you're thinking, "I had that joy once but now it's gone. How can I get it back?"

WHAT CAN YOU DO TO CULTIVATE JOY?

The first thing you need to do is you need to make it a priority to pursue this holy joy. It is, after all, part of the goal of your salvation. We are commanded to seek joy and delight for ourselves. We need to make it a priority in our worship, our personal study, and in our prayer and solitude. This joy comes from believing in our sovereign God and in trusting Him to keep His promises to us. Promises like, "He who began a good work in you is faithful and will carry it to completion" (Philippians 1:6). And "I know the plans I have for you. To prosper you and not to harm you. Plans to give you a hope and a future" (Jeremiah 29:11). And "No one who trusts in the Lord will ever be put to shame" (Psalm 25:3).

These are the promises of God the Father Almighty, maker of heaven and earth, to every person who comes to Him through Jesus Christ. Nothing can keep God from keeping those promises to you. Do you believe that? Does that show in your life? In your relationships? In your commitments? In your priorities? Your joy will strengthen or weaken depending on how you answer those questions.

When I get down, or depressed, or spiritually dry, when I can't seem to keep hold of my joy, I have a number of songs, hymns, books, and sermons that I listen to that get refocused on God, His holiness, His greatness, and His grace and love.

Let me share with you one of my favorites. It is a praising of God by a minister named S.M. Lockridge. He is now worshiping with the saints in heaven. But for the last twenty years I have listened to this fantastic message. Whenever I become spiritually joyless I pull out this message and the joy begins to run back into my soul. It is still available to hear on the internet. If you have the capability to download and hear him give this message, I highly recommend it. But it is just as powerful in print. I close this chapter with it in its entirety. May God use it to help you grow and cultivate your joy.

> My King was born King. The Bible says He's a Seven Way King. He's the King of the Jews – that's a racial King. He's the King of Israel – that's a National King. He's the King of righteousness. He's the King of the ages. He's the King of Heaven. He's the King of glory. He's the King of kings and He is the Lord of lords.
>
> Now that's my King. Well I wonder if you know Him. Do you know Him? Don't try to mislead me. Do you know my King?
>
> David said the Heavens declare the glory of God, and the firmament show His handiwork. My King is the only one whom there are no means of measure

can define His limitless love. No far seeing telescope can bring into visibility the coastline of His shore of supplies. No barriers can hinder Him from pouring out His blessing.

Well, well, He's enduringly strong. He's entirely sincere. He's eternally steadfast. He's immortally graceful. He's imperially powerful. He's impartially merciful. That's my King.

He's God's Son. He's the sinner's savior. He's the centerpiece of civilization. He stands alone in Himself. He's august. He's unique. He's unparalleled. He's unprecedented. He's supreme. He's pre-eminent.

Well, He's the loftiest idea in literature. He's the highest personality in philosophy. He's the supreme problem in higher criticism. He's the fundamental doctrine of true theology. He's the cardinal necessity of spiritual religion. That's my King. He's the miracle of the age. He's the superlative of everything good that you choose to call Him.

Well, He's the only one able to supply all of our needs simultaneously. He supplies strength for the weak. He's available for the tempted and the tried. He sympathizes and He saves. He's strong God and He guides. He heals the sick. He cleanses the lepers. He forgives sinners. He discharged debtors. He delivers the captives. He defends the feeble. He blesses the young. He serves the unfortunate. He regards the aged. He rewards the diligent and He beautifies the meek. Do you know Him?

Well, my King is the key of knowledge. He's the

wellspring of wisdom. He's the doorway of deliverance. He's the pathway of peace. He's the roadway of righteousness. He's the highway of holiness. He's the gateway of glory. He's the master of the mighty. He's the captain of the conquerors. He's the head of the herocs. He's the leader of the legislatures. He's the overseer of the overcomers. He's the governor of governors. He's the prince of princes. He's the King of kings and He's the Lord of lords. That's my King. Yeah. Yeah. That's my King. My King, yeah.

His office is manifold. His promise is sure. His light is matchless. His goodness is limitless. His mercy is everlasting. His love never changes. His Word is enough. His grace is sufficient. His reign is righteous. His yoke is easy and His burden is light.

Well, I wish I could describe Him to you, but He's indescribable. He's indescribable. Yes. He's incomprehensible. He's invincible. He's irresistible. I'm coming to tell you, the heavens of heavens cannot contain Him, let alone a man explaining Him. You can't get Him out of your mind. You can't get Him off of your hands. You can't outlive Him and you can't live without Him.

Well, Pharisees couldn't stand Him, but they found out they couldn't stop Him. Pilot couldn't find any fault in Him. The witnesses couldn't get their testimonies to agree. Herod couldn't kill Him. Death couldn't handle Him and the grave couldn't hold Him. That's my King. Yeah.

He always has been and He always will be. I'm

talking about He had no predecessor and He'll have no successor. There was nobody before Him and there'll be nobody after Him. You can't impeach Him and He's not going to resign. That's my King! That's my King! Thine is the kingdom and the power and the glory. Well, all the power belongs to my King. We're around here talking about black power and white power and green power, but it's God's power. Thine is the power. Yeah. And the glory. We try to get prestige and honor and glory for ourselves, but the glory is all His. Yes. Thine is the Kingdom and the power and glory, forever and ever and ever and ever. How long is that? And ever and ever and ever and ever. And when you get through with all of the evers, then, Amen.

FREEDOM UNDER SOVEREIGNTY MEANS

The Bible is full of promises of joy, commands to be joyful and to rejoice, descriptions of believers as being full of joy, exhortations not to lose joy, and encouragements to keep and even to increase our joy.

Jesus died not only to forgive you, but to bring you joy.

Growing in joy is part of the goal of your faith.

Joy is the automatic response to the sure hope of our future glory with Christ.

This joy is the joy of being with God and enjoying Him in the same way that Jesus enjoys His Father.

Joy outlasts happiness. It is much more powerful and far more enduring than happiness.

Our joy comes from believing in the sovereignty of God and in trusting Him to keep His promises to us.

VERSE TO REMEMBER

You love him even though you have never seen him. Though you do not see him now, you trust him; and you rejoice with a glorious, inexpressible joy.
1 Peter 1:8

LEARNING TO LIVE UNDER SOVEREIGNTY

1. Why does Jonathan Edwards believe that affections like joy are essential to a healthy spiritual life? Do you agree? Why or Why not?
2. When you are in church do you see a room filled with joyful Christians? If you answered "no," how would you describe the people who attend your church?
3. Can you identify with the Christians Peter is writing to in 1 Peter 1:8-9? Explain.
4. Jesus did not only die to forgive you, He died to bring you joy. Where does this joy come from?

5. How is joy different from happiness?
6. What are some of the enemies of joy in life?
7. How can you defend yourself against them to protect your joy?
8. Can you experience joy even when you are experiencing seasons of great difficulty? Why or why not?
9. How does a healthy belief in the sovereignty of God help us to cultivate a life of joy?
10. What is one habit that you can identify that you need to give up that gets in the way of cultivating joy in your life?
11. What is one thing you can commit to changing in your life this week that will help cultivate your joy?

CULTIVATING FREEDOM UNDER SOVEREIGNTY

One of the most important lessons I have been learning from Peter's description of the Christians he was writing to in 1 Peter is that they were full of joy even in the midst of the pain and suffering of oppression. It does not mean we never experience grief, anger, or frustration. The joy that Christ promises us exists in spite of those feelings. This is a very important acknowledgment that Peter makes. We need to know that joy is not going to come instead of hard times but will be there through hard times. What are some things you might be able to do to keep your eyes out for joy even when life is hard?

I shared in this chapter that when I am not feeling joy in my life I have songs, hymns, books, and sermons that I listen to that get me refocused on God, His holiness, His greatness, and His grace and love. Make a list of what can help you to keep the feeling of joy alive in your heart.

Two of the best books to read about the place and importance of joy in the Christian life are *Religious Affections* by Jonathan Edwards and *Desiring God: Mediations of a Christian Hedonist* by John Piper. *Religious Affections* is also available in a condensed modern English book titled *The Experience that Counts*. I highly recommend these two books.

C h a p t e r   6

REST FROM FEAR OF FAILURE

You will trample upon lions and cobras; you will crush fierce lions and serpents under your feet!

PSALM 91:13

The Holy Spirit helps our infirmities, but he does not encourage our idleness; he loves active believers. Who are the most useful men in the Christian church? The men who do what they undertake for God with all their hearts. Who are the most successful Sabbath-school teachers? The most talented? No; the most zealous; the men whose hearts are on fire, those are the men who see their Lord riding forth prosperously in the majesty of his salvation. Whole-heartedness shows itself in perseverance; there may be failure at first, but the earnest worker will say, "It is the Lord's work, and it must be done; my Lord has bidden me do it, and in his strength I will accomplish it."

C.H. SPURGEON, *MORNING AND EVENING*,
MORNING MARCH 15

Psychologists have given names to almost every fear under the sun. For example, if you have a fear of...

...crowds—then you have *ochlophobia*.

...darkness—you have *nyctophobia*.

...being looked at by other people—you have *scopophobia*.

...loneliness—you have *monophobia*.

…marriage—you have *gamophobia*.

…poverty—you have *peniaphobia*.

…school—yep, you guessed it, *schoolphobia*.

…God—theophobia.

…death—thanataphobia.

…hell—hadephobia.

…failure—you have *kakorrhaphiophobia*.

Isn't it ironic that the very term for having a fear of failure is such a long and unnatural word that you will most likely fail in trying to pronounce it? Talk about adding insult to injury!

If being anxious is fear of what might happen *to* you, the fear of failure is a fear that you will fail to successfully accomplish anything God wants you to do. Sometimes we become so afraid of what we might do wrong, or of losing what we have, that we end up doing nothing at all.

No one can avoid failure all the time. Failure finds us all. And when it does it can be crushing. You know what I am talking about. Failure in handling our financial obligations. Mistakes we've made as parents that have wounded our relationships with our kids. Failure with our spouse that led to divorce. Failure to resist the lure of extramarital sex that has left you hating yourself. Continually failing at keeping our promises whether it be as simple as being on time, or as serious as giving up drugs or alcohol. After the fear of death, the fear of failure is the most common phobia people struggle with today.

I remember a time several years ago when my wife and I were living in New Jersey when I really struggled with the fear of failure. That year failure seemed to follow me around like my shadow. I could not get away from it. First, I was laid off from my job as a teacher. I got a job at a telecom company in accounts payable, worked real hard and did real well but was laid off from there too. Then I got a job at the temp agency that got me my job, and I was laid off from that job!

I had just spent seven years getting a three-year degree so that I could go into pastoral ministry. I was struggling with trying to juggle the requirements of my presbytery to complete their ordination requirements. I was struggling to provide for my family. I had no leads on ministry work because I had not yet completed the ordination requirements.

I was miserable. I was failing at ordained ministry and I hadn't even started yet! I felt that I was failing as a husband and as the provider. And being completely honest, living in Trenton, New Jersey was no help to my overall mood either!

I remember walking into a Barnes and Noble store one day during this time and saw on display a copy of John Maxwell's book, *Failing Forward*. I bought the book on the spot. I have read many books by Maxwell but that one has been by far the most helpful book of his that I have read.

But it wasn't what helped me the most. What helped me the most was learning what the Bible says about the causes and cures for the fear of failure. Simply said, what I have been learning is when we struggle with the fear of failure we are not resting in the sovereign power and provision of God's grace, or in His promise to give us all we need to do His work. The place God brought me to so I could begin understanding this was Peter's denial of Jesus.

THE SETUP

The disciples are reclining with Jesus at the table in the upper room, finishing what would be their last Passover together. Jesus breaks the bread and blesses the cup and transforms the meaning and significance of Passover into its full meaning as the sacrament of communion.

The disciples know that something is up. Jesus is not acting like Himself. He is obviously sad and struggling with something very heavy in His mind and heart. Then as if things weren't weird enough already, Jesus suddenly blurts out that one of the men sitting with them at the table was going to betray Him. If there was confusion before, there was outright bewilderment now. Who among them could possibly do such a thing?

After dinner, as they were walking to the Mount of Olives, Jesus lobbed another grenade into the already emotionally charged atmosphere of the disciples. "Tonight all of you will desert me," Jesus told them. "For the Scriptures say, 'God will strike the Shepherd, and the sheep of the flock will be scattered'" (Matthew 26:31). This was the last straw. The disciples couldn't believe what Jesus was saying. Their pride could not handle such a harsh critique of their faith in Jesus. Peter was first to say what was on all the other disciples' minds.

> Peter declared, "Even if everyone else deserts you, I never will."
>
> "Peter," Jesus replied, "the truth is, this very night, before the rooster crows, you will deny me three times."
>
> "No!" Peter insisted. "Not even if I have to die with you! I will never deny you!" And all the other disciples vowed the same (Matthew 26:33-35).

THE FAILURE

Now let's fast forward a few hours. Jesus has been arrested in Gethsemane. Judas betrayed him. All the disciples, as Jesus had foretold, had run for their lives. Peter, however, followed Jesus' captors back to the Temple where He was brought before Caiaphas, the High Priest, to be tried on charges of blasphemy. In Matthew 26:69 we pick up the story with Peter hovering as close as he felt he could to Jesus without being noticed.

> Meanwhile, as Peter was sitting outside in the courtyard, a servant girl came over and said to him, "You were one of those with Jesus the Galilean."

> But Peter denied it in front of everyone. "I don't know what you are talking about," he said.

> Later, out by the gate, another servant girl noticed him and said to those standing around, "This man was with Jesus of Nazareth."

> Again Peter denied it, this time with an oath. "I don't even know the man," he said.

> A little later some other bystanders came over to him and said, "You must be one of them; we can tell by your Galilean accent."

> Peter said, "I swear by God, I don't know the man." And immediately the rooster crowed. Suddenly, Jesus' words flashed through Peter's mind: "Before the rooster crows, you will deny me three times." And he went away, crying bitterly.

Can you imagine how Peter felt? He wanted to be so strong for his friend Jesus. He went so far as to swear to Jesus before all the disciples, "Even if I have to die with you, I will never disown you." And you know what? I think he meant it. He wanted to do what all the other disciples did not do.

But he flunked!

Not only did he have the pain of failing, he had the added pain of knowing that Jesus *knew* he was going to fail. How many of us in hindsight have said "If I only knew what was going to happen as a result of my actions, I would have done everything differently!" He knew the future and still could not change it! How horrible did Peter feel! It is times like these when we fail so miserably, that we create in ourselves the fear that we cannot be trusted to accomplish anything. We lose trust in ourselves.

But something much more insidious happens as the fear of failure begins to take hold within us. We start to doubt God. We start to doubt His love for us. His promises to be faithful and gracious and to provide all we need begin to fade from our memories until we are left with the idea that we would never be called to do anything for God, great or small, because God would never risk His success by trusting failures like us with His business.

God has given you a shield to defend yourself against such fear. Fear of failure is defeated by trusting in the sovereignty of God. We need to understand that all forms of the fear of failure are rooted in the unbelief of God's sovereign grace and faithfulness.

WHY DOES GOD LOVE YOU?

God's love, joy, and commitment to you are in no way based on your successes and are in no way compromised by your failures. You need to understand the basis on which you are loved and accepted as a child of God. You are accepted because of Jesus Christ. Not because of anything you have done or not done. Ephesians 2:8-9 makes this very clear, "For it is by grace you have been saved, through faith—and this not from yourselves, it is the gift of God—not by works, so that no one can boast." It doesn't matter how good you are or how many successes you've had. That's not why God loves you.

That is one of the most important lessons that our failures can teach us: there is nothing in us that deserves God's favor. Our failures help us grow a real humility and an honest assessment of ourselves before God. Failure helps us to acknowledge our weakness and helplessness. We become convinced of how much we need God because we are so prone to failure. Failure brings us to God and puts us in a position to let God work in our lives in such a way as to make us realize that He gets all the glory.

It has to be by grace. God's grace and faithfulness are not given to you because you earned it. They are given because God made a promise to be committed to you because of His commitment to Christ.

You do not have to worry about losing God's love because of your failures. You are no different than Peter. Jesus knew Peter was going to deny Him three times. Jesus *knew* Peter was going to fail! He knew Peter was going to fall flat on his face. Jesus told him He knew.

What did the angels tell the women who first came to the empty tomb? "But go, tell his disciples *and Peter*, 'He is going ahead of you into Galilee. There you will see him, just as he told you'" (Mark 16:7, ESV emphasis added). In the parallel telling of Peter's denial of Jesus in the Gospel of Luke, right before Jesus predicts Peter's denial, Jesus says to him, "Simon, Simon, Satan has asked to sift you as wheat. But I have prayed for you, Simon, that your faith may not fail. And when you have turned back, strengthen your brothers" (Luke 22:32, ESV). Jesus was praying for him and was spiritually protecting him *even knowing that he was going to fail.* Jesus' only request was that he take his experience of God's grace and faithfulness and share it with his fellow believers

95

and so strengthen his brothers in Christ.

Jesus is praying that same way for each of us. Jesus is *always* interceding for you before the Father. Satan may desire to sift you like wheat, but Jesus has been and will continue to pray for you, that your faith may not fail.

GOD WORKS THROUGH WEAKNESS AND FAILURE

God has promised to be faithful to you so there is no need to fear failure. The reason we don't need to be afraid of failure is because our sovereign God has promised to be faithful to us. Look at how God addresses our fear. He says in Deuteronomy 31:6, "Be strong and courageous. Do not be afraid or terrified because of them, for the LORD your God goes with you; *he will never leave you nor forsake you*." He says in Lamentations 3:22-23, "Because of the LORD'S great love we are not consumed, for his compassions never fail. They are new every morning; *great is your faithfulness*." And in 1 Corinthians 1:8-9 God says, "He will keep you strong to the end, so that you will be blameless on the day of our Lord Jesus Christ. God, who has called you into fellowship with his Son Jesus Christ our Lord, *is faithful*" (emphasis mine).

By grace, God uses us in spite of our failures, not because we are free from failures. We need to understand that God sovereignly works through our weaknesses and even our helplessness to accomplish the work He has given us to do.

God is not expecting us to do, or become, or save in our own strength. God assures us that no matter how big the task, how bleak the circumstances, or how useless we feel, the Holy Spirit is going to work through us so that we will do everything the Father has planned for us to do. Our confidence comes from God's abilities, God's resources, and God's strength, not ours.

God wants you to know that you don't have to be afraid of failing at what God wants you to do. He has promised to be with you wherever you go. God is never going to leave you. He is never going to forsake you. He is always going to be with you wherever you go. We don't need to worry about failing because God has promised to give us everything we need and to do all that needs doing so that He will accomplish His work through us.

FREEDOM UNDER SOVEREIGNTY MEANS

No one can avoid failure all the time. Failure is part of life.

When we struggle with the fear of failure, we are not resting in the sovereign power and provision of God's grace, or in His promise to give us all we need to do His work.

God's love, joy, and commitment to you are in no way based on your successes and are in no way compromised by your failures.

Jesus is always interceding for you before the Father. Satan may desire to sift you like wheat, but Jesus has been and will continue to pray for you, that your faith may not fail.

Our confidence comes from God's abilities, God's resources, and God's strength, not ours.

VERSE TO REMEMBER

So be strong and courageous! Do not be afraid and do not panic before them. For the LORD your God will personally go ahead of you. He will neither fail you nor abandon you.
Deuteronomy 31:6

LEARNING TO LIVE UNDER SOVEREIGNTY

1. What is the fear of failure?
2. Why is the fear of failure so common?
3. Why is it not a good thing to try and avoid failure altogether in our lives?
4. How can our failures be used to help us grow in our relationship with God?
5. What is God's love for us and commitment to us based on? What is it not based on?
6. How can developing a healthy humility help us overcome the fear of failure?

7. Read the following passages that tell us of God's commitment to be faithful to us: Deuteronomy 31:6, Lamentations 3:22-23, and 1 Corinthians 1:8-9. What help do these passages offer to a person struggling with the fear of failure? Which passage means the most to you and why?

8. Psalm 121:1-2 (ESV) says, "I lift up my eyes to the hills. From where does my help come? My help comes from the Lord, who made heaven and earth." Do you look to God for your help or do you look to yourself and your own resources?

9. What keeps you from depending on God for your help?

10. What is one step you can commit to making this week to help you increase your trust in God's promise to be faithful to you?

11. If you really struggle with the fear of failure, who is someone you could get together with to help you grow in this area. Make a note of that person's name and contact them this week.

CULTIVATING FREEDOM UNDER SOVEREIGNTY

I shared in this chapter about a time in my life when failure seemed to follow me around like a shadow. The two things that really helped me overcome that growing fear of failure were reading *Failing Forward* by John Maxwell and prayerfully reading Scripture. One of the lessons I began learning at that time was that failure was not so much a sign of uselessness as it was a natural part of personal and spiritual growth. Think about how you view failure in your life and in the lives of others. Permission to fail is one of the healthiest things you can give at home or in your business or at your church. What might you be able to do to help create an atmosphere where failure is seen as something to learn from and grow from instead of something to avoid?

Get a copy of *Failing Forward* by John Maxwell at your library or bookstore.

Consider reading about people in the Bible like Abraham, Moses, Saul, David, and Jonah who struggled with failure. If you are a pastor or leader in your church, consider a small group study or sermon series on how God used these people because of or in spite of their failures.

Chapter 7

FREEDOM TO LIVE BOLDLY

The wicked run away when no one is chasing them, but the godly are as bold as lions.

PROVERBS 28:1

In like manner, Christ's people must "go forth unto him." They must take their position "without the camp," as witness-bearers for the truth. They must be prepared to tread the straight and narrow path. They must have bold, unflinching, lion-like hearts, loving Christ first, and his truth next, and Christ and his truth beyond all the world. Jesus would have his people "go forth without the camp" for their own sanctification. You cannot grow in grace to any high degree while you are conformed to the world. The life of separation may be a path of sorrow, but it is the highway of safety; and though the separated life may cost you many pangs, and make every day a battle, yet it is a happy life after all.

C.H. SPURGEON, *MORNING AND EVENING*,
MORNING APRIL 6

At the National Prayer Breakfast, Washington, D.C, February 5, 1994. Mother Teresa dared to say what no one there dared to say. In doing so, she received a standing ovation from the majority gathered for the occasion. It was an address repeated for weeks on radio, TV, and print. Here is a portion of the text of her address.

> I was surprised in the West to see so many young boys and girls given to drugs. And I tried to find out why. Why is it like that, when those in the West have so many more things than those in the East? And the answer was: 'Because there is no one in the family to receive them.' Our children depend on us for everything — their health, their nutrition, their security, their coming to know and love God. For all of this, they look to us with trust, hope and expectation. But often father and mother are so busy they have no time for their children, or perhaps they are not even married or have given up on their marriage. So their children go to the streets and get involved in drugs or other things. We are talking of love of the child, which is where love and peace must begin. These are the things that break peace.

> But I feel that the greatest destroyer of peace today is abortion, because it is a war against the child, a direct killing of the innocent child, murder by the mother herself. And if we accept that a mother can kill even her own child, how can we tell other people not to kill one another? How do we persuade a woman not to have an abortion? As always, we must persuade her with love and we remind ourselves that love means to be willing to give until it hurts. Jesus gave even His life to love us. So, the mother who is thinking of abortion, should be helped to love, that is, to give until it hurts her plans, or her free time, to respect the life of her child. The father of that child, whoever he is, must

also give until it hurts.

By abortion, the mother does not learn to love, but kills even her own child to solve her problems. And, by abortion, that father is told that he does not have to take any responsibility at all for the child he has brought into the world. The father is likely to put other women into the same trouble. So abortion just leads to more abortion. Any country that accepts abortion is not teaching its people to love, but to use any violence to get what they want. This is why the greatest destroyer of love and peace is abortion…

And for this I appeal in India and I appeal everywhere — "Let us bring the child back." The child is God's gift to the family. Each child is created in the special image and likeness of God for greater things — to love and to be loved. In this year of the family we must bring the child back to the center of our care and concern. This is the only way that our world can survive because our children are the only hope for the future. As older people are called to God, only their children can take their places…

Please don't kill the child. I want the child. Please give me the child. I am willing to accept any child who would be aborted and to give that child to a married couple who will love the child and be loved by the child. From our children's home in Calcutta alone, we have saved over 3000 children from abortion. These children have brought such love and joy to their adopting parents and have grown up so full of love and joy.[3]

That's bold!

What you may not realize is that you have been wired by the Holy Spirit to be filled with the same boldness that filled Mother Teresa that morning. We need to realize that we have been freed to have the same boldness. In fact Proverbs 28:1 says, "The wicked run away when no one is chasing them, but the godly are as bold as lions." In Christ we have been given a new life that sets us free to be as bold as lions.

WHAT KEEPS US FROM BEING BOLD

There are many words that I have heard people use to describe Christians. Christians have been described in my hearing as being hypocrites, judgmental, and as narrow minded. I have *never* heard someone say, "You know what, Christians are a bold bunch of people!" Boldness is a quality that seems exceptionally rare among God's people today. Why do so few seem to attain the boldness described in Proverbs 28:1?

The well-known gospel singer Whitley Phipps said, "The biggest chink in the Christian's armor today is that he thinks God is important—but not everything." I believe that he hit the nail on the head. We put *some* level of confidence in God, we put *some* level of trust in God, we submit in *some* respect to God, but we do not often go *all the way*. God is important, God is powerful, God is faithful but God is not everything, God is not all-powerful, and God is not absolutely dependable. When your God is important but not everything, you are not going to let go of other things that are important to you. When you believe that God is powerful, but not all-powerful, you are not going to confidently enter the place where you know you are weak. When you believe God is faithful but not absolutely dependable, you are not going to live with the courage and boldness of a lion. Instead, you conclude that the effort will not be worth it.

We simply do not want to pay the cost of obedience. The cost may be comfort. The cost may be relationships. The cost may be the esteem of others. This comes from not placing our relationship with God above all else. Fear keeps us from being bold. We fear rejection. We fear the repercussions. We fear we will get in over our heads. We don't have confidence in ourselves.

WHY WE CAN BE BOLD

The key to boldness is confidence in God's sovereign power to provide all we need to do His will. Boldness comes from confidence. If you are not confident, you cannot be bold. We can be bold in our living and loving and working and witness and relationships because God is in control.

One of the great promises in the Bible is in the book of Isaiah 26:3 where he says, "He will keep in perfect peace all who trust in you, all whose thoughts are fixed on you!" How many of you like the idea of God keeping you in perfect peace? What does peace mean here? What is God promising? It's important to know because we could each have different ideas of what that means.

Sometimes it's easier to explain what something means by saying what it isn't. Let me tell you what peace does not mean. The peace God is talking about here does not mean the absence of problems, or trouble, or challenges. God never promises that in this life. Where do we get this idea that God wants you to be happy all the time? What Jew or Christian in the Bible ever experienced anything close to that? Even Jesus' life was full of ups and downs, surprises and disappointments, challenges, and heartaches. Why should we expect to experience anything different? Peace does not mean the absence of trials or problems.

The perfect peace that God offers here is a peace that you have even in times of trial or pain. It is a peace that comes from knowing that God, the creator of heaven and earth, loves you and He is the one who is in control over everything in the universe.

This peace comes from trusting that God is sovereignly good. There used to be a poster downstairs in the kitchen at the church where I pastor that said, "I will be handling all your problems today. I will not need your help. –God." Wouldn't it be great if you knew that God, that God the Father Almighty, was working in your life to assure that you were going to get where you needed to go, and do all the things He had for you to do? That no matter what was going on, no matter what bombs go off in your life that you are going to make it because God has promised to get you there? That is peace. That peace is the key to confidence in God that frees us to live life boldly.

There are two qualifications given in that verse that we need to have in order to take advantage of the benefits of this promise of peace that frees us to be courageous in all things.

YOU HAVE TO HAVE YOUR MIND FIXED ON HIM

What a thought, to have your mind fixed on Him. That means to have your mind and your heart leaning on and resting in God. It means to fully depend on God. The mind is an incredible thing. How you think is the key to understanding where you are in life and it is the key to changing where you are.

Where you are is a result of your actions. Your actions are the result of your choices. Your choices are a direct result of your attitudes. Your attitudes are a direct result of how you think. Where is your mind? What are you focused on? What are you thinking about? Where you choose to fix your mind is the single greatest factor over which you have any real control in your life.

There is a lot in life that you cannot control, but you can control what your mind is fixed on. Jesus said it like this in Matthew 6:21, "Wherever your treasure is, there the desires of your heart will also be." Your treasure is whatever you are fixed on.

To be fixed on God means to depend on Him, to look to Him for what you need, for help to get through the valleys of life so you come out the other side better and sweeter instead of sour and bitter. It means trusting in Him even when you don't understand what He is doing, or why He is allowing things to happen as they do. It means fixing your mind on the fact that He is God and He knows what He is doing and where He is leading you and why you need to go the way He is bringing you.

YOU HAVE TO TRUST GOD

That's really what it comes down to, isn't it? I think the reason so many Christians struggle with living boldly comes from the fact that we don't really trust God. We talk the talk but we don't walk the walk. We think that for some reason God isn't trustworthy.

The number one reason we have trouble trusting God is that we want to trust God on our terms. Let me give you an example of what I mean.

My daughter Maggie loves the snow. This winter (the winter of 2006-7) has been very disappointing to her because it has been so snow-less here in Boston. At least several times a week for the last few months (as far back as

October) she has asked me, "Daddy, is it going to snow today?" My answer has most often been, "No, honey, it is too warm for it to snow." A few weeks ago she started to pray for it to snow. She prays like this, "God, could You please make it snow?" then she pauses for a few seconds with her eyes scrunched shut then opens them and exclaims, "He said, 'Yes.'"

Well, she wakes up the next morning and looks out the window and is all disappointed that there is no snow. Last week she came up to my wife Mandi and asked, "Why doesn't God answer my prayers?" I'm tempted to say with my fatherly sarcasm, "He did, dear. You asked Him if He could make it snow and He answered you right away. He said 'Yes,' remember? Next time be sure to ask Him if He *would* make it snow." Or "He did Maggie, but you did not specify where you wanted it to snow so Denver is now buried under two feet of snow. Next time try and be more specific, OK?"

What concerns me about her question is that it tells me that she is starting to wonder what she can trust God with. If He won't answer her prayer to make it snow, what else will He not answer?

That is building our trust on our terms. "If You do this for me I will start to trust you." "If You heal me or heal my friend of this illness, I will start to trust you." "If You remove this problem from me, I will start to trust You." God wants us to trust Him on *His* terms. God's answer to our desire to trust Him on our own terms is clearly answered in Paul's request to heal him of his "thorn in the flesh."

In 2 Corinthians 12:9 God answered Paul saying, "My grace is all you need. My power works best in weakness." God is saying, "You don't need to be free of this problem or that problem to have trust in Me. You don't need to be healed of your disease or have your limitations removed to be useful to Me. My grace is enough. I am enough. My glory and power shine the brightest when I work through you in spite of your weakness, not in removing your weakness. I know what I am doing. Trust Me."

That is the $64,000 question: do you trust Him? Have you trusted yourself totally to Jesus? Do you trust God in the big things as well as in the small things? How do you go about doing that? How do you go about building trust in God so that He is not just important, but everything?

In Philippians 4:6-7 God says, "Don't worry about anything; instead, pray about everything. Tell God what you need, and thank him for all he has done. Then you will experience God's peace, which exceeds anything we can understand. His peace will guard your hearts and minds as you live in Christ Jesus." Here are four things God wants you to do so that you will be free to live boldly and confidently in the peace of God.

DON'T WORRY ABOUT ANYTHING

That's God's polite way of saying, "Remember that there is someone in control of the world and it's not you." God is in charge and He loves you and will provide for you. Not just a little, but everything you will need. Not everything you want, but everything you need to both become all He wants you to be, and to accomplish all he wants you to do.

There is no person, no power, no circumstance, and no combination of any of those that can even come close to challenging the power of God the Father Almighty in your life. In Jeremiah 29:11 God promises, "I know the plans I have for you," says the LORD. "They are plans for good and not for disaster, to give you a future and a hope."

Nothing can keep God from doing all the good He plans for those He loves.

PRAY ABOUT EVERYTHING

Nothing can keep your prayers from being heard by God. Psalm 9:10 says, "Those who know your name trust in you, for you, O LORD, do not abandon those who search for you." God is always listening to our prayers. He always hears us. That gives us great confidence. Not only are we always in God's grasp, but God is always within our reach. He is never far off. Sometimes we feel that way. Sometimes we feel that God is nowhere to be found. But we need to know that this is not the case.

Just because fog might keep me from seeing the trees outside my window, I know that they are still there. Just because the clouds hide the sun, even for days at a time, I know the sun is still there. We never need to worry that our prayers will fail to be heard. We never need to worry that our cries for help will not reach His courts. He is completely trustworthy. God never abandons those who search for Him. Nothing can stop God from hearing or answering our prayers and helping us in our times of need. He will always prove faithful because He is sovereign.

TELL GOD WHAT YOU NEED

Nothing can keep God from providing for you, and helping you. Psalm 57:3 says, "He will send help from heaven to rescue me, disgracing those who hound me... My God will send forth his unfailing love and faithfulness." Isaiah 41:10 says, "Don't be afraid, for I am with you. Don't be discouraged, for I am your God. I will strengthen you and help you. I will hold you up with my victorious right hand." When God hears one of his children cry out for help nothing can keep him from coming to their aid. Nothing! But you say sometimes I pray and nothing seems to happen, help does not come right away. Let me tell you something, just because you don't see it coming does not mean it isn't. Let me give you two scriptures that illustrate this.

Look at Daniel 10:12. Daniel began praying for wisdom to understand a dream that God had given him. Daniel was so distraught by what he saw that he fasted and did not even perfume himself. The first day went by. Then a second. Then a third. This continues for three whole weeks! Then while Daniel is walking down the streets of Babylon along the shore of the Tigris River, an angel appears to Daniel and says,

> Don't be afraid, Daniel. Since the first day you began to pray for understanding and to humble yourself before your God, your request has been heard in heaven. I have come in answer to your prayer.

The moment Daniel started to pray, God heard His prayer and set in motion the forces of the spiritual realms to answer Daniel's prayer. But Daniel did not know what God was doing until the angel of God revealed it to him. To the human eye it appeared that a lot of time and effort and self-denial was being answered with God's silence, but what we learn is that Daniel's consistent and persistent prayers were of great import in the spiritual world. In the next verse the angel continues, "But for twenty-one days the spirit prince of the kingdom of Persia blocked my way. Then Michael, one of the archangels, came to help me, and I left him there with the spirit prince of the kingdom of Persia." There was spiritual warfare being waged behind the scenes. And the clear implication is that it was Daniel's praying for three weeks that were used by God to be the occasion of Michael's coming to overpower the spirit of Persia, that this angel might be free to come to Daniel and give him the interpretation of his vision.

And consider 2 Kings 6:15-17. The king of Aram wanted to attack Israel. But every time he made plans, the Lord revealed his plans to Elisha who told them to the king so that Israel was always ready to counter Aram's armies. The king of Aram was furious and asked who among his men was committing treason by helping Israel. They told the king that the problem was not a traitor, but the prophet Elisha in Israel who was hearing everything from God. The king of Aram found that Elisha was living in Dothan and sent his army to surround the city. This time they did.

Elisha had with him a servant. This servant had no doubt been with Elisha as he received all these communications from God with which his master successfully warned the king of Israel and foiled the armies of Aram. But this day, the servant woke up and went to the window and was shocked by what he saw. The city was surrounded by a huge army of Aramenians. The armies of Israel were nowhere in sight. We read in 2 Kings 6:15-17,

> When the servant of the man of God got up early the next morning and went outside, there were troops, horses, and chariots everywhere. "Oh, sir, what will we do now?" the young man cried to Elisha. "Don't be afraid!" Elisha told him. "For there are more on our side than on theirs!" Then Elisha prayed, "O LORD, open his eyes and let him see!" The LORD opened the young man's eyes, and when he looked up, he saw that the hillside around Elisha was filled with horses and chariots of fire.

To the human eye things looked grim. They looked impossible. They looked like God had left His servant Elisha to be killed. But when you saw the situation with spiritual eyes, you saw that nothing could be further from the truth. This army that looked so invincible was about to get creamed by the heavenly armies of God the Father Almighty. It did not look like God was working, but God was as active and protective as ever.

Nothing can keep God from providing for you. There is no power than can stop Him, or hinder Him, or trick Him.

Jesus promised in John 14:14 to provide for you saying, "Ask for anything in my name, and I will do it, because the work of the Son brings glory to the Father." Nothing can stop God from providing all that we need in order to do everything He has planned for us to do and to become all He wants us to be in Christ.

BE THANKFUL FOR WHAT HE HAS GIVEN YOU

A great place to start is with your own salvation and forgiveness. God declares in Isaiah 45:21-22, "there is no other God but me—a just God and a Savior—no, not one! Let all the world look to me for salvation! For I am God; there is no other." Because God is sovereign nothing can take us away from God's grace and forgiveness. "Nothing in all creation will ever be able to separate us from the love of God that is revealed in Christ Jesus our Lord." Nothing can separate us from His love because God is sovereign. Because He is sovereign we can have absolute faith that He will do all that He promises.

When we live in the confidence of those promises we experience the freedom that Christ purchased for us at the cross. When we rest in the absolute trustworthiness of those promises we will gladly submit our lives, our ambitions, our

113

dreams, our talents, all that we are and all that we have to the work and power of the Spirit. When we live in the assurance of these promises, we are free to trust God in ways and in situations that we never thought possible.

When you do those things, you are training your mind to be fixed on Him and you will grow in your trust in Him. Then you will experience God's peace, which exceeds anything we can understand. His peace will guard your hearts and minds as you live in Christ Jesus.

When we believe that God planned us for His work to serve Him and He called us and set us aside to do it, we can have the confidence to take risks to do God's work. Let me share with you three reasons why you should have unshakable confidence in God's promise to come through for you.

NOTHING CAN CHANGE YOUR POSITION BEFORE GOD

No matter what happens, no matter who tries or what powers might conspire, nothing can change your position before God. Nothing can separate you from the love of God. We can be bold in this world for Christ because we know that we are safe in Christ's love. We do not need to worry about falling out of God's love. Christ is holding on to us and nothing can take us from His hand. We no longer look to the approval of people for our direction or self-worth. This gives us God-grounded confidence. We no longer need to be afraid of what people think because we are not living for people, we are living for God.

Because of God's sovereign grace and unshakable promise of faithfulness, we are not only freed *from* the fear of failure, we have been *freed to* live boldly. We are free to attempt things that we know we would never be able to do or accomplish on our own. And we don't have to be afraid because we have the unshakable promise of God's grace and God's faithfulness backing us up. 2 Timothy 1:7 tells us that "God did not give us a spirit of fear but of power and love and self-control."

God knew Joshua needed to be free from the fear of failure and have the freedom in his faith and leadership to be bold so He encouraged him in Joshua 1:9 saying, "Have I not commanded you? Be strong and courageous. Do not be terrified; do not be discouraged, for the LORD your God will be with you wherever you go."

When God spoke to Jeremiah and revealed that he had been called to be a prophet, Jeremiah was scared and unsure of himself or his abilities. He did not think he could do it. He was too young. He was not a good speaker. So God spoke to him in Jeremiah 1:8 saying, "Do not be afraid of them, for I am with you and will rescue you, declares the LORD."

You can be bold in standing up for your faith and telling the good news to anyone because Jesus said, make up your mind not to worry beforehand how you will defend yourselves. For I will give you words and wisdom that none of your adversaries will be able to resist or contradict (Luke 21:14-15).

The reason for our boldness is not based in our strength. Our reason for boldness is not hindered by our weaknesses or shortcomings. Our boldness is grounded in Christ and on God's promises to glorify Himself through us. When we are about the Father's business we have been promised that we will be given everything we need to do our part in God's work. This is a very important distinction. The boldness we have been freed for is not for doing anything we want. It is for doing what God wants us doing.

You can take risks that the world sees as foolish because God wants to do great things through you. Because "God chose the foolish things of the world to shame the wise; God chose the weak things of the world to shame the strong. He chose the lowly things of this world and the despised things—and the things that are not—to nullify the things that are, so that no one may boast before him. It is because of him that you are in Christ Jesus, who has become for us wisdom from God—that is, our righteousness, holiness and redemption. Therefore, as it is written: "Let him who boasts boast in the Lord" (1 Corinthians 1:27-31).

God uses the weak to show His strength. He uses imperfect people to accomplish His perfect will. When God works through us, through our failures, and through us in spite of our inadequacies, there is no question that what was accomplished was accomplished in the power of God. He gets all the glory due his name. And we get all the joy of having seen God work through us and with us to accomplish His great purposes. That is awesome!

You have been freed from the prison of fear and have been given the freedom to risk and be bold. So get out there and do not be afraid, because the Lord your God has spoken to you saying, "Be strong and courageous. Do not be afraid or terrified, for the LORD your God goes with you; he will never leave you nor forsake you."

FREEDOM UNDER SOVEREIGNTY MEANS

The biggest chink in the Christian's armor today is that he thinks God is important—but not everything.

The key to boldness is confidence in God's sovereign power to provide all we need to do His will.

To be fixed on God means to depend on Him, to look to Him for what you need, for help to get through the valleys of life so you come out the other side better and sweeter instead of sour and bitter.

God is in charge and He loves you and will provide for you. Not just a little, but everything you will need.

God is always listening to our prayers. He always hears us. Not only are we always in God's grasp but God is always within our reach.

We no longer look to the approval of people for our direction or self-worth. This gives us God-grounded confidence. We no longer need to be afraid of what people think because we are not living for people, we are living for God.

God uses the weak to show His strength. He uses imperfect people to accomplish His perfect will. When God works through us, through our failures, and through us in spite of our inadequacies, there is no question that what was accomplished was accomplished in the power of God.

VERSE TO REMEMBER

The wicked run away when no one is chasing them, but the godly are as bold as lions.
Proverbs 28:1

LEARNING TO LIVE UNDER SOVEREIGNTY

1. Do you know any Christians you would describe as "bold as a lion" for God? Who are they and how have

117

they shown boldness?

2. In your experience, what have you seen that keeps people from being bold?

3. In what ways do people show that God is important but not everything?

4. What two things does a person need to do in order to experience the "perfect peace" God promises in Isaiah 26:3?

5. How can having the peace that Isaiah 26:3 promises help us to live boldly?

6. What are some examples of people basing their trust in God on their own terms?

7. Why does God want us to trust Him on His own terms?

8. Read Daniel 10:12 and 2 Kings 6:15-17. What do these passages teach us about prayer?

9. We are encouraged to be bold even when we feel we are weak or not suited to the task (2 Corinthians 12:9). Why does God want us to be bold even when He does not give us all the talent or abilities to do His work ourselves?

10. How can living boldly help you in your marriage, at work, and at church? What can you do to encourage others in your family, church, or small group to live boldly this week?

CULTIVATING FREEDOM UNDER SOVEREIGNTY

I shared in this chapter how my daughter Maggie was struggling with what she could trust God with because He did not answer her prayers for snow in the time and manner she wanted. I think most of us would agree that her concern was based on an immature picture of God and prayer. Many pastors and Christian leaders today want to do great things for God and set about to do them and then ask God to bless what they are doing. That is really doing the same thing—wanting to build trust in God on our own terms. Boldness comes from knowing you are doing what God wants you doing for His kingdom. It does not come from doing what you want to be doing for God's kingdom and asking Him to bless your plans. Set aside some significant time, preferably a whole day or even a weekend that you can spend in prayer seeking God's discernment about your own plans for your work, family, church, or ministry. Are you asking God to bless your plans, or are you seeking God's blessing so you can implement His plans?

While God uses imperfect people to accomplish His perfect will, He also works through our natural talents and spiritual gifts to get things done. Have you ever thought about what your gifts are? If you haven't ever done so, consider taking a spiritual gifts assessment or a strengths assessment. It is important to have a clear idea about how God has gifted you so that you can discern the place God has for you in His kingdom. I highly recommend assessments from *Personality Insights* and *Leading from your Strengths*.

It is just as important to know your weaknesses as it is to know your strengths. What are the things that keep you from trusting God so that you can boldly follow Him and obey Him in your home or ministry? Write them down. Once you have them written down, pick the one that gives you the most trouble and ask God in prayer to help you make a simple plan to overcome that fear. This should not be a plan to get rid of that weakness, but a plan to help you trust God and live boldly in spite of that weakness.

Chapter 8

REST FROM SHAME

The LORD says, "I will rescue those who love me. I will protect those who trust in my name. When they call on me, I will answer; I will be with them in trouble. I will rescue and honor them.

PSALM 91:14-15

They who wear the white robe in heaven overcame through the blood of the Lamb, and we may do the same. No lust is too mighty, no besetting sin too strongly entrenched; we can overcome through the power of Christ. Do believe it, Christian, that thy sin is a condemned thing. It may kick and struggle, but it is doomed to die. God has written condemnation across its brow. Christ has crucified it, "nailing it to his cross." Go now and mortify it, and the Lord help you to live to his praise, for sin with all its guilt, shame, and fear, is gone.

C.H. SPURGEON, *MORNING AND EVENING*,
MORNING JULY 27

LESSONS FROM SEATTLE

Seattle is a great modern city. Starbucks is based there. It's got the Space Needle. But Seattle has a secret. Seattle is not built on the ground.

You would never know it by looking at it now, but Seattle was originally built on a swamp. Americans have always been willing to try anything…even building cities on swamps. But because the city was built on such wet ground and right at water level, the citizens of Seattle had continual problems with plumbing and sewage backing up… occasionally even shooting back up out of the toilet!

Then in 1889 a great fire burned twenty-five blocks of the city to the ground. Instead of rebuilding the city, the people of Seattle decided to rebuild up. The city of Seattle as we know it and see it today is actually built two stories above the ground. The great looking modern city is hiding an old broken down city that is built on a swamp.

There was no way to get rid of the swamp or the burned remains of the city at the time, so it was left buried under the new one. Most of it is inaccessible to the public, although the homeless often find their way down there to get out of the weather. There are, however, still parts of the underground city which you can take tours of today.

WHAT ARE WE HIDING?

Many of us are hiding something on the inside. Many of us might look like we have everything altogether on the outside, but on the inside we are hiding the fact that we know there is a lot of swampy ground inside us. Author Steve Brown has said that we all have something inside us that if it became public would move us to jump off a bridge. Do you identify with that? We are hiding the fact that we have buried inside us failures and brokenness. We keep these things buried deep in our soul where no one goes and no one can see. Some of them sank into the swamp. Some of them were burned. All we know is that we can't fix it and we can't get away from it. The most we can do is try to ignore it.

The awful truth is that those sins, failures, hurts, and

pains often end up seeping out into the rest of our souls, don't they? Sometimes we just can't seem to get away from feeling that we are more than just broken. Sometimes we come to the conclusion we are beyond repair. That feeling is shame.

DEFINITION OF SHAME

Shame is a feeling that leaves us believing that we are worthless, hopeless, and that we are a disgrace. It is jumping from the belief that we do bad things, into the belief that we are bad to the core and are beyond repair. When shame has a hold on us, we are convinced that we are unable to do anything for God because we have nothing to offer Him. God would do nothing for us because we are too broken for Him to waste His time and energy on.

Shame is a different feeling from feeling guilt. Guilt says "I do bad things." Shame goes a step further. Shame says, "I am bad." It is one thing to feel ashamed over something bad that we have done. That is a healthy feeling of shame. But when the feeling of shame starts to go beyond that into a chronic feeling that starts to dominate our thinking about ourselves we get into a different ball game altogether.

There was a prophet in Old Testament times whose name was Jeremiah. Much of his ministry was giving bad news to people; and the people he had to give it to did not know that you should not take out your anger on the person who delivered it! Even though he was a man of God who walked with God and talked with God, he struggled with shame. He said, "Why did I ever come out of the womb to see trouble and sorrow and to end my days in shame?" (Jeremiah 20:17-18, NIV).

GETTING OUT FROM UNDER THE SHADOW OF SHAME

Our sin should bring us to the conclusion that we are broken beyond repair. That is the reason Christ died for us. When we accepted Jesus as our Savior, that shame for our sinful nature was removed by God's merciful love.

What do you do when you are being dogged by shame? You could ask that question to a thousand different people and get 1001 answers, but a year from now only one of them is going to do you any good, and that's the answer that you get in Psalm 34:5, "Those who look to God for help will be radiant with joy; no shadow of shame will darken their faces." What a promise! No shadow of shame will darken the faces of those who look to God.

The fact that God is sovereign means that God made each of us *on* purpose, *for* a purpose, in His image. We can give up shame because we are all necessary parts of God's creation, and necessary people in the Body of Christ, the Church.

YOU HAVE WORTH AS A CREATION OF GOD

All that God creates has worth. He created you on purpose, for a purpose. Psalm 115:3 says, "Our God is in the heavens; He does all that he pleases. (ESV)" That means that God only does what He wants. If God only does what He wants, that means that God wanted to create you. It pleased Him to create you. God took the time and care to think about who your parents would be so that you would have the exact genetic makeup that God wanted you to have. Psalm 139:13-16 tells us that God personally and intentionally created you.

You made all the delicate, inner parts of my body

and knit me together in my mother's womb. Thank you for making me so wonderfully complex! Your workmanship is marvelous—how well I know it. You watched me as I was being formed in utter seclusion, as I was woven together in the dark of the womb. You saw me before I was born. Every day of my life was recorded in your book. Every moment was laid out before a single day had passed.

Choosing your parents, where you would be born, what you would look like, what kind of personality you would have, and what you would do pleased God and brought Him pleasure.

Jonathan Edwards, in a sermon titled *A Watchman's Great Concern for Souls*, made a profound insight into the care God took to make you and the worth you have as one of His creations.

God is the creator of men in both soul and body; but their souls are in a special and more immediate manner His workmanship, wherein less use is made of second causes, instruments or means, or anything pre-existent. The bodies of men, though they are indeed God's work, yet they are formed by Him in a way of propagation from their natural parents, and the substance of which they are constituted is matter that was pre-existent; but the souls of men are by God's immediate creation and infusion, being in no part communicated from earthly parents, nor formed out of any matter or principles existing before.[4]

It pleased God to make you. Out of nothing, in the same manner He created the world out of nothing, God spoke your name and created an immortal soul that would be perfectly served by your physical body. You bring God joy! And that means you have great worth. Once you start thinking about this fact, that God is sovereign and only does what pleases Him, you cannot help but see the incredible worth you have as a creation of God's. Everything God does is an expression of His perfect wisdom, goodness, and power. The very fact that you are here and reading this book implies that had God not created you, His creation would not be as good or perfect or as much an expression of His power! You are a unique and necessary part of God's creation.

YOU HAVE GREATER WORTH BEING MADE IN THE IMAGE OF GOD.

You have great worth as an intentional creation of God's. Genesis 1:26-27 tells us that there is something more special about being a human being.

> Then God said, "Let us make human beings in our image, to be like ourselves. They will reign over the fish in the sea, the birds in the sky, the livestock, all the wild animals on the earth, and the small animals that scurry along the ground." So God created human beings in his own image. In the image of God he created them; male and female he created them.

You have even more worth being a person who is made in His image.

What does it mean to be made in the image of God? Being made in God's image doesn't have anything to do with our physical bodies or with how we look or sound. God is spirit (John 4:24). God's image is found in our soul, the very part of each of us that is handcrafted out of

125

nothing but God's pleasure. It is our soul that bears the likeness of God. Like God we can be creative, we can reason, we have a similar capacity to act with the same affections that God has such as love, grace, goodness, mercy, and compassion. Bearing His image means that God can communicate to with us, and we with Him. It means we can be in a relationship with Him and appreciate His love for us and express our love for Him. As God rules and has authority over His creation, making us in His image means that we have authority to rule and care for and love the world God created for us (Genesis 1:26). We are God's physical ambassadors in this world, for this world.

Being made in the image of God, we are both the height of God's creation and are the subject of God's special care and planning. Edwards says in the same sermon,

> And as the souls of men are more directly from God, by the more special and immediate exercise of His divine power as a creator, and are what He challenges as His by a special propriety, and are the most noble part of the lower creation, and are infinitely distinguished from all other creatures here below in that they are immortal beings; so they are, above all other creatures which God hath made in this world, the subject of God's care and special providence.[5]

We know this from Romans 8:28-30, "And we know that God causes everything to work together for the good of those who love God and are called according to his purpose for them. For God knew his people in advance, and he chose them to become like his Son, so that his Son would be the firstborn among many brothers and sisters. And having chosen them, he called them to come to him. And having called them, he gave them right standing with himself. And having given them right standing, he gave them his glory." God's love for you as a believer in Christ influences everything He does in this world. Everything God does He does for His own glory. He glorifies Himself by saving you that His "Son would be the firstborn among many brothers and sisters." Everything God orders, allows, and brings to pass through His sovereign power aims to prove His love to His Son and to you and to all those whom He has chosen as His own by bringing you into the full possession of His glory.

YOU HAVE GREATER WORTH BECAUSE GOD GAVE HIS SON THAT YOU MIGHT BE REDEEMED TO HIM.

God knows that you have been broken and that you struggle with sin, failures, guilt, and shame. Yet as a creation of His, and having an immortal soul that bears His image, you have great worth to God. And to show you how great He is and how much worth He places on you, He sent His Son Jesus to secure salvation for you. God has shown you love in the most extreme, intimate, and costly way. That love meant going all the way to the cross. Jesus' death on the cross paid the penalty for our sins and made forgiveness certain for all who trust in Jesus as their Savior. Again Edwards writes,

> Each soul is infinitely more precious than all the precious gems the earth affords... You may judge how much Christ [values]...the souls of men, by what He has done and suffered for them: He has shown how precious He has judged immortal souls to be, in that He, though a person of infinite glory, did not think His own blood, His life, His soul, too precious to be offered up as a price for them to

redeem them, that they might obtain…salvation.[6]

You are worth so much to God that He did not hesitate to pay for your redemption with the very life of His Son, the most valuable possession God has. If you trust in Jesus there is nothing left keeping you from knowing the love of God who knows how much you are worth. In Jesus, we have been given a sure hope that no matter what our circumstances may presently be, God has promised to never leave us or forsake us.

AS HIS CHILD YOU HAVE GREAT WORTH BECAUSE HE LOVES YOU AS HIS OWN SON.

You are loved, blessed, and accepted by God perfectly in Christ. There is nothing you can do to make God love you more. And there is nothing you can do to make Him love you less. John 17:22-23 is one of the most amazing verses in the Bible. Listen to what it says,

> I have given them the glory that You gave me, that they may be one as we are one: I in them and You in me. May they be brought to complete unity to let the world know that You sent me *and have loved them even as You have loved me* (emphasis added).

Did you catch that? God loves you as much as He loves Jesus! Can you even imagine that? Can you comprehend that? You can't be more loved than that. You can't be loved more than God loves you right now at this moment.

Friend, have you not yet come to know the love and grace of your heavenly Father? You can change that right now. All that takes is admitting what you already know to be true. It is true that you are broken. Sin has broken all of us. It is true that you cannot fix yourself. You cannot get rid of the mess or clean out the dirt and muck that seems to be so much a part of you.

Give your shame to God. Tell God that you accept the love He offers you through Jesus. That is all it takes to begin the end of the power of shame in your life. The love of God is a mortal wound to shame. Once you own the fact that you cannot fix yourself, God will do for you what you are unable to do for yourself. He will wipe away your shame with His love. And your name "I am worthless" will be changed to "I have great worth." Your name "I am hopeless" will be changed to "I have hope." And your name "I am a disgrace" will be replaced with "I am loved."

FREEDOM UNDER SOVEREIGNTY MEANS

You deal with guilt with forgiveness. The way you cure shame is with love.

Psalm 115:3 says "Our God is in the heavens and all that He pleases He does." That means that God only does what He wants. It pleased Him to create you. You bring God joy, and that means you have great worth.

God knows that you have been broken and that you struggle with sin, failures, guilt, and shame. And to show you how great He is and how much worth He places on you as His creation, He sent His Son Jesus to secure hope for you.

God loves you as much as He loves Jesus! You can't be more loved than that.

VERSE TO REMEMBER

Those who look to him for help will be radiant with joy; no shadow of shame will darken their faces.

Psalm 34:5

LEARNING TO LIVE UNDER SOVEREIGNTY

1. What is the difference between guilt and shame?
2. We are all created in the image of God. What does that mean?
3. What are some ways that people hide their shame?
4. What are some ways you have seen shame affect people you know?
5. Read Psalm 34:5, 115:3, and 139:13-16. What do these verses tell us about God? How can each of these passages help us to deal with our shame?
6. Read Romans 8:28-30. What promises does God make in this passage? To whom are they made? How do these promises help us to battle shame?

7.   Jonathan Edwards wrote, "the souls of men are by God's immediate creation and infusion, being in no part communicated from earthly parents, nor formed out of any matter or principles existing before." How does knowing that God created your soul out of nothing effect your self worth in light of your answers to question 5?

8.   Are there circumstances or challenges currently in your life that keep you from knowing how much you are loved by God? What is it about those challenges that keeps you from trusting in God's love for you?

9.   What are some ways that God has acted in your life that reveal His love for you?

10.   What is one step you can commit to this week to help you increase your trust in God's love for you?

CULTIVATING FREEDOM UNDER SOVEREIGNTY

The spiritual medicine for guilt is forgiveness. The medicine for shame is love. When we come across a person who is struggling with shame it often means learning to love that person in spite of some ugly and painful realities that they have buried inside them. This is one of the hardest lessons God teaches us about loving others. God wants us to show love that does not cringe at the brokenness or swampy mess we see in them. One of the things I have been learning is that loving people in spite of perceived unloveliness, becomes a lesson about how God loves me despite my own darkness of soul. Think about how you respond to people who are struggling with shame. Do you distance yourself from them? Do you show disgust and distain for them once the reason for their shame is exposed? Honestly ask if you are loving people with this struggle with the same love God gives to you every day.

One of the ways to help people open up about their own struggle with shame is to open yourself up about how you have struggled with shame. The more transparent you are about yourself, the more people will be willing to take off their masks with you and be transparent themselves. This opens the door to helping them see through your example that God loves them perfectly and that they have great worth.

Shame is an issue that many people in the church struggle with today, but it is rarely dealt with from the pulpit. If you are a pastor, consider a message on dealing with shame. Also, make a list of people in your congregation who have a gift for encouraging and valuing others and connect them to people who are struggling with shame.

Chapter 9

FREEDOM TO LOVE

I have loved you, my people, with an everlasting love. With unfailing love I have drawn you to myself.

JEREMIAH 31:3

Grow also in love. Ask that your love may become extended, more intense, more practical, influencing every thought, word, and deed.

C.H. SPURGEON, *MORNING AND EVENING*,
MORNING JANUARY 4

The old saying goes, "love makes the world go round." If that's true it is not always obvious, is it? Love is hard, isn't it? Love is hard to define. It's hard to figure out. It is hard to know what the reason for loving a thing should be. When you hear "love makes the world go round" you don't hear a lot of disagreement from people. But when you look around, you wonder if love really does make the world go round. Is anyone really loving? My friend and mentor R.C. Sproul once said, "When someone introduces himself or herself with the words, 'I need to tell you something in Christian love,' what follows is usually not Christian nor loving!" You have to ask yourself, do we really know what love is?

More than half of all marriages end in divorce.

40% of families do not have a father living at home.

1500 ministers leave the ministry every month because

133

they just can't handle the lack of love in themselves or in their congregations (or their congregations can't handle the lack of love in them).

But every once in a while we see or hear about someone that defies our common experience, people like Billy Graham and Mother Teresa. They stand out so dramatically that they are almost impossible to ignore.

How do you love like that? What frees a person to love without counting the cost, to love in spite of oppression, to love the seemingly unlovable?

LOVE IS LEARNED

The way a person loves is completely learned from the love a person is given. Love is a learned thing. What it means, how you show it, is all learned. If your experience with love is that it centers around good and happy feelings, that is how you will determine what love is and how to show it. If you want to experience the kind of love that makes the world go round, you need to know and experience the love of the Man who makes the world go round.

Listen to what Jesus said to His disciples in John 15:9-17:

I have loved you even as the Father has loved me. Remain in my love. When you obey my commandments, you remain in my love, just as I obey my Father's commandments and remain in his love. I have told you these things so that you will be filled with my joy. Yes, your joy will overflow! This is my commandment: Love each other in the same way I have loved you. There is no greater love than to lay down one's life for one's friends. You are my friends if you do what I command. I no longer call you slaves, because a master doesn't confide in his slaves. Now you are my friends, since I have told you everything the Father told me. You didn't choose me. I chose you. I appointed you to go and produce lasting fruit, so that the Father will give you whatever you ask for, using my name. This is my command: Love each other.

Jesus learned how to love from His Father. Jesus loved people with a love like no one had experienced in another person before. That one Person's love has changed the entire world. He gave that same love to his disciples with the intention of having them *share that same love with others.* The awesome truth contained in these verses is that Jesus wants to enable you to love in the same way He loves people, "Love each other in the same way I have loved you."

When we experience the love of Jesus we become freed from shallow and selfish counterfeits of love, to authentically love others with the love with which He loves us. What Jesus did for us was free us to live a life of divine God-centered, God-empowered love. We are freed to love what God loves and we can love people the way God loves them. Jesus' love frees us and transforms our ability to love in three ways.

JESUS FREES US TO LOVE GOD.

We don't need to be afraid of God. We do need to fear God, but we don't need to be afraid of God. Proverbs 1:7 says, "Fear of the LORD is the foundation of true knowledge." The fear we are supposed to have is a reverence, a respect, an acknowledgement of the holiness and greatness of God. Whenever a people in the Bible encountered God in His glory in the Bible, they fell to the ground, they covered their eyes. They were moved to say with Isaiah, "Woe is me! For I am lost; for I am a man of unclean lips, and I dwell in the midst of a people of unclean lips; for my eyes have seen the King, the Lord of hosts!" (Isaiah 6:5, ESV).

In C.S. Lewis' classic, *The Lion, The Witch, and the Wardrobe*, the main characters Peter, Susan, Edmund, and Lucy are told they are going to be brought to see the King of Narnia, the Son of the Great Emperor across the Sea. And they are told he is a lion. Susan, ever the example of the practical young woman asks, "Is he safe?" I love the reply she is given, "Safe! Who said anything about safe! Of course he isn't safe, but he's good." God isn't safe. We need to fear Him. We would be stupid not to. But God is also good. He is love. He is Your Father.

A gentleman who thought Christianity was merely a heap of puzzling problems, said to an old minister, "That is a very strange statement, 'Jacob have I loved, but Esau have I hated.' "Very strange," replied the minister; "but what is it that you see most strange about it?"

"Oh, that part, of course, about hating Esau."

"Well, sir," said the minister, "how wonderfully are we made and how differently constituted! The strangest part of all to me is that He could ever have loved Jacob. There is no mystery so glorious as the mystery of God's love."[7]

We don't need to worry about earning or keeping His approval. We are loved by God because of who we are in Christ, not because of anything we have done. We are His sons. We are His daughters. And because of that we don't need to be afraid of Him.

I have three daughters. I am the only male living in my house. I am a minority in a sorority. I love being a dad, and I love my girls. I love them because God made me their dad. I love them because they are my children. No matter what they have done or will do in the future, nothing will change the fact that I am their dad and that they are God's gifts to me. I will always love them. My love for them is not based on what they do, it is based in who they are.

That is the reason God loves His children. It is not based on what we do, though God certainly is not pleased with all that we do. His love for you is based on who you are in Christ. That love frees us to love God and trust God and depend on God in the same way that Jesus did. That is awesome freedom.

JESUS FREES US TO LOVE OURSELVES.

Self-love is basic to being human. It is one of the ways in which we are created in the image of God. God loves Himself and so seeks His own glory and happiness in all He does. This is the clear implication of Psalm 115:3, "Our God is in the heavens, and he does as he wishes." The word the NLT translates *wishes* in the original Hebrew means pleases, delights, desires, favors, or likes. So God not only does whatever He wishes, but more specially He does whatever He pleases or whatever brings Him pleasure so that the ESV translates the same verse, "Our God is in the heavens; he does all that he pleases."

Jonathan Edwards had a wonderfully simple definition of self-love. He said that self-love is nothing more than loving your own happiness.[8] He said, "That a man should love his own happiness is necessary to his nature, as a faculty of will is; and it is impossible that it should be destroyed in any other way than by destroying his being."[9] Loving yourself is a central part of what it means to be a person made in the image of God. If you take away that self-love, you take away a key part of what makes us human.

The mandate for having a healthy love of self is clearly implied in the second part of the great commandment, "love your neighbor *as yourself*" (Matthew 22:39). Edwards observed that

> Scripture from one end of the Bible to the other is full of things which are there held forth to work upon a principle of self-love. Such are all the promises and threatenings of the Word of God, and all its calls and invitations; its counsels to seek our own good, and its warnings to beware of misery. Which things can have influence upon us in no other way than as they tend to work upon our hope or fear. To what purpose would it be to make and promises of happiness, or denounce any threatenings of misery, to him who neither loved his own happiness nor hated his own misery? Or to invite and counsel him to seek the one, or warn him to avoid the other?[10]

If it is the nature of how God made us to love ourselves, then how does God's love free us to love ourselves? It frees us by opening our hearts and minds to where our greatest joy is—in loving God! Our greatest love, our highest joy comes from knowing, relating, and loving God. God's love for us first frees us to love Him and by doing so He frees us to love ourselves.

Because of sin, our self-love became disconnected from God's love. As a result the self-love we have apart from God is only concerned with ourselves. It is self-centered. It is selfish. After the fall of Adam our love shrank and became myopic. We cannot see or appreciate showing love that is not rooted in our own self-interest and benefit. In essence our self-love has no compass, no guide to regulate it in relation to anything outside of us and our personal interests.

God's love restores our self-love to its original design, being built upon the foundation of the love of our Creator and Father. Far from being decreased, God wants us to see that in loving Him, enjoying Him, and glorifying Him, our love for ourselves is increased and augmented. Loving God is seeking your greatest good, and therefore to love yourself and to pursue your own happiness to its fullest you need to find your joy in God. Edwards says,

> A man may love his own happiness as much as anybody, and may be in an high exercise of love to his own happiness, earnestly longing after happiness, and yet he may place that happiness that he may in the same act be in an high exercise of love to God. As for instance, when the happiness for which he longs is to enjoy God, and to behold the glory of God, or to enjoy communion with God. Or a man may place his happiness in glorifying God; it may seem the greatest happiness to him that he can conceive of to give Glory as he ought to do, and he may long for this happiness. If he did not love what he esteemed his happiness he would not long for it. And to love his happiness is to love himself. But yet in the same act he loves God, because he places his happiness in God. What can more properly be called love to any being, or any thing, than to place one's happiness in that thing?[11]

You love yourself the best when you love what brings you the most joy and happiness. God's love frees you to love yourself in the highest capacity possible.

Living a life of love reveals the spring of joy that Christ has with the Father. "I have told you these things so that you will be filled with my joy." His joy was to love people with the love He had been given by the Father. When we begin learning to love that way, we begin learning about the joy that Jesus promises.

JESUS FREES US TO LOVE OTHERS

You begin to find that your love for God drives you to pursue your happiness in the happiness of others. God's love in us brings us to love ourselves and then flows out from us to love others with that same love. Again, let me quote Jonathan Edwards.

> Selfishness is a principle which does, as it were, confine a man's heart to himself. Love enlarges it and extends it to others. A man's self is as it were extended and enlarged by love. Others so far as beloved do, as it were, become parts of himself; so that wherein their interest is promoted he looks on his own as promoted, and wherein their interest is touched his is touched.[12]

When you start loving the way Jesus loves you realize the truth of Jesus' promise, "It is more blessed to give than to receive." Being free to love means being free to give others the love that is flowing from the Source of Love in your soul. It means being free to love others by giving your time, free to love others by sharing your talents, free to be generous with your money and possessions. It means being free to love when it is hard as well as when it is easy, free to love when it is inconvenient as easily as when it is convenient, free to love when it is costly as easily as when it is affordable.

That is the real difference between what many people think of as love and the love that makes the world go round, isn't it? It is that kind of love that made Mother Teresa spend her life on the orphans of India. It is that kind of love that drives Jesus to leave the flock of ninety-nine to find the one that is lost. It is that kind of love that Jesus followed to the cross so that He might have the joy of bringing you forgiveness and freedom. He knew we were trapped by our sin. He knew that we could not break free ourselves. And for no other reason than love He freed us so that we could live with Him, in Him, and for Him and know the joy that He has in the Father.

That same love is now a part of you because of the work of the Holy Spirit in your heart. And God does not want you to keep it to yourself as if it were in limited supply. He wants you to love with the same passion with which He loves you. "This is my commandment: Love each other in the same way I have loved you."

Your Father wanted you to be free to live a life of love. Jesus purchased that freedom for you with His life. The Holy Spirit has connected you to the Father so that you know His love, so that you know where your happiness lies; that you may love yourself, and in that same love that Christ has for you, you experience an overflow of that love that moves you to live a life of love for your family, your friends, your fellow Christians, your neighbors, and even your enemies.

FREEDOM UNDER SOVEREIGNTY MEANS

The way a person loves is completely learned from the love a person is given. Love is a learned thing. What it means, how you show it, is all learned.

When we experience the love of Jesus we are free to love the way He loves us.

God's love for you is based on who you are in Christ. That love frees us to love God and trust God and depend on God in the same way that Jesus did.

When we understand that God loves us as He loves His Son, we are free to love ourselves.

We are free to love people because God loves those people. Not because they are perfect. Not because they are obviously lovely to us, but because they are lovely to God.

VERSE TO REMEMBER

I have loved you, my people, with an everlasting love. With unfailing love I have drawn you to myself.
Jeremiah 31:3

LEARNING TO LIVE UNDER SOVEREIGNTY

1. Do you believe the old saying, "love makes the world go round?" Why or why not?
2. Read John 15:9-17. In your own words, what was Jesus teaching His disciples (and us)?
3. What are the three ways we are freed to love through Jesus Christ?
4. Which of those ways do you feel that you are best at? Which one is the most difficult for you? Why?
5. Do you think you can learn to love the way God loves? Why or why not?
6. What are some examples from your life that show you that God loves you?

7. Jesus says in John 15 that Jesus' joy was in loving people with the same love He had received from His Father. His command to us is that we do the same thing for others. What keeps us from loving other people the way God loves us? Why is it so hard?

8. We all know people who are very difficult to love. Have you ever shown love to a person who was very difficult to love? Was it a positive experience or a negative one?

9. What can we do to help ourselves love people who most people consider to be unlovable?

10. Who do you know who needs to know God's love? Write their name down and begin praying for God to reveal His love to them. What can you do to show God's love to them this week?

CULTIVATING FREEDOM UNDER SOVEREIGNTY

One of the key thoughts in this chapter is that how we show love to others is learned by how we have been loved ourselves. A good question to ask yourself and other leaders in your church or ministry is: how are people learning to love from you? We teach what we know, but we reproduce what we are. If people in your family, church, or ministry are not loving people with the love that Jesus loves them with, what can you do to change that?

It is important that the people you are leading at home or at church know that God's love for them is based on who they are in Christ, not on their actions. Spend time conveying this truth to your people.

God's love moves you to share that love with others. If you don't see this going on where you are leading, you will need to provide some opportunities for your people to start learning this. At our church we have started Thanksgiving and Easter dinners which we put on for the poor and elderly and lonely in our community; and our youth serve hot chocolate to people waiting at the bus stop in town. What are some ideas you could come up with to give the opportunity to share God's love with others?

Chapter 10

REST FROM GUILT

I will reward them with a long life and give them my salvation.

PSALM 91:16

Come, my soul, think thou of this. Believing in Jesus, thou art actually and effectually cleared from guilt; thou art led out of thy prison. Thou art no more in fetters as a bond-slave; thou art delivered now from the bondage of the law; thou art freed from sin, and canst walk at large as a freeman, thy Savior's blood has procured thy full discharge. Thou hast a right now to approach thy Father's throne. No flames of vengeance are there to scare thee now; no fiery sword; justice cannot smite the innocent.

C.H. SPURGEON, MORNING AND EVENING,
MORNING FEBRUARY 13

My first paper in college needed to be based on an opinion poll. Being the mature college man that I was, I decided to ask people to pick who was their favorite superhero—Superman or Spiderman.

Who do you think won? Spiderman won. Does that surprise you? Two out of every three people I asked picked Spiderman over Superman. When I asked "Why Spiderman?" I really only got one answer: he was easier to identify with. He seemed more real.

I have personally always been a big Spidy fan. In fact, I

am an avid reader of the Ultimate Spiderman comic book series. I have received several Spiderman Christmas tree ornaments from members of my church. I have used illustrations from the Spiderman movies in my sermons several times. I think the reason the story is still such a draw today is still the same as it was when I wrote my college paper. Peter Parker, a.k.a. Spiderman, is someone we can identify with very well.

Why?

One of the things that we really identify with is Peter Parker's struggle with guilt. Guilt is something we all have. Guilt comes from two different sources.

The Sin we Commit

Guilt comes from doing things we know we shouldn't have done. Many times guilt comes from things we deliberately did which we knew were wrong. But guilt can also come from things we should not have done that were unintentional; bad decisions that we made in the heat of the moment.

Good that we Omitted

Perhaps a more insidious cause of guilt comes from not doing what we knew we should have done. This is where a lot of Peter Parker's guilt comes from. Deciding not to stop a thief he knew was passing by him because he wanted revenge against the person the thief had robbed, resulted in that thief killing his Uncle Ben who was raising him. That guilt drove him to become Spiderman. His uncle's counsel, "with great power comes great responsibility" became his motto.

But being Spiderman came with its own consequences. Since all his spare time was spent being Spiderman, he began to fail as a student and all his relationships began to deteriorate.

In Spiderman 2, Peter's guilt over losing these friendships and not living up to his potential as a student in college drove him to give up his life as a superhero. But that too had great consequences. In one of the most powerful scenes in the movie, Peter walks by a mugging. He sees it happening. He hears the man being mugged cry for help. He knows he has the power to save him. But he walks away. As he does, you can feel the weight of the guilt growing on his face.

We all identify with Peter Parker because we have all been where he is. We have all done things that we regret doing. We have all made choices that in retrospect were so clearly selfish and caused so much pain to the people around us that we marvel at how stupid and blind we can be.

All of us have guilt, but not everybody deals with it in the same way. There are really only three ways that we can deal with our guilt.

WE CAN DENY IT.

We all know President Harry Truman's famous declaration, "The Buck Stops Here." Sadly, few people seem to claim that moral standard for themselves. Time after time we hear on the news, reality shows, talk shows, and documentaries about people who do not want to accept personal responsibility for their actions. One blames their parents. Another blames alcohol. Another blames illness. Some people even say "the devil made me do it." We can deny our guilt all we want. But the denial of guilt does not remove or negate it.

Do not think that denying guilt is a product of modern times. It is as old as the human race. Adam ate the forbidden fruit and his first instinct was to deny his guilt.

> [T]he LORD God asked. "Have you eaten the fruit I commanded you not to eat?"
>
> "Yes," Adam admitted, "but it was the woman you gave me who brought me the fruit, and I ate it."
>
> Then the LORD God asked the woman, "How could you do such a thing?"
>
> "The serpent tricked me," she replied. "That's why I ate it" (Genesis 3:11-14).

The very first sin Adam and Eve committed after the fall was attempting to rationalize their guilt away. The definition of rationalize is to tell yourself *rational lies*. You can deny your guilt all you want. It doesn't change the fact that you have your share. If you don't believe me just ask your wife! Don't have a wife? Just ask your mother, she'll set you straight!

WE CAN BURY IT.

I was watching *Law and Order: Criminal Intent* recently. I love the character of Mike Logan on that show. On this particular episode, Logan shoots and kills an undercover cop. Even though he is cleared from any wrongdoing since the undercover cop did not identify himself and would not lower his gun, Logan was wracked with guilt for killing an innocent man and fellow police officer.

Eventually, Logan shows up at the office of one of the police psychologists. She tries to assure him that everything is OK and that he did everything right. She said, "You have to accept that sometimes you can do everything right and still end up with a bad result." Logan leans forward and knowing he is not going to like what he hears asks, "How?

How am I supposed to accept that?" Her reply, "You learn to deal with it...over time." Logan rolled his eyes at her answer. What she was telling him to do was just bury it.

Unfortunately this is the message many people get from counselors, psychologists, and psychiatrists today. We can learn to *cope* with guilt by learning new ways of thinking, or we can learn to *manage* the painful feelings of guilt with prescription drugs. Coping is one thing, but being *free* of guilt is something else.

Others try to bury their guilt in more harmful ways by turning to alcohol, illegal drugs, or other harmful behaviors.

Still others try to bury their guilt under good works. Since we can't take back what we've done that causes the guilt we have, we attempt to do as much good as we can to cover our guilt so that it no longer matters. This is one of the key struggles of Peter Parker in the Spiderman story. Like Peter Parker, we tell ourselves all the good we are doing will certainly outweigh our guilt.

WE CAN LET IT BURY US

Martin Luther almost let his guilt bury him. Before his revelation that we are saved by faith not by works, he went to confession every day. He was so guilt-ridden by his sins he would almost have gone every hour.

On most nights Luther slept well, but he even felt guilty about that, thinking, "Here am I, sinful as I am, having a good night's sleep." So he would confess that. One day the priest to whom Luther went for confession said to him, "Martin, either find a new sin and commit it, or quit coming to see me!"

Like Martin Luther, sometimes we start to let our guilt define who we are. Unresolved guilt eats away at us. It eats away at our self-esteem and self-worth until we think that we are worthless, helpless, hopeless.

I think a great illustration of this feeling is how the police officers who were pulled from the rubble of the World Trade Center after the 9/11 attacks must have felt. Buried alive and pinned under a skyscraper of rubble, unable to move. Some people end up simply resigning themselves to the weight of the guilt they feel upon them; there is nothing they can do except to wait for the inevitable. These all have one obvious thing in common: they don't get rid of guilt. When enough guilt builds up inside you, it starts to take on any number of outer forms.

REGRET.

Many people today are struggling with the regret that they did not do things differently in life. One example of this is a poll that was taken in 1999. This poll asked people of all ages if they could start over in life, would they choose to do things "much differently?" The results may surprise you.

Ages 16-31: 59%

Ages 32-50: 71%

Ages 51+: 59%[13]

Many of us carry a large load of regret about our past that is rooted in the guilt we have for the mistakes we've made, poor decisions, rash judgments, and selfish choices we have made.

DEPRESSION

When we cannot get free from our guilt, we easily become depressed. We start to think that nothing good is ever going to come in life either because we won't deserve it, or we are too weak to bring about any good.

FEAR

Chronic feelings of guilt can lead to great increases of fear. We start to worry that God is out to get us and make us pay for all our mistakes. This fear leads us to assume the worst and question anything that appears to be good.

Guilt can lead to a fear of inadequacy and failure that ends up paralyzing us, keeping us from doing what we know we need to be doing because we are so afraid that we will fail again and end up with more guilt. Fear drives us to conclude that it is safer to do nothing than deal with the possibility of acquiring more guilt.

HOPELESSNESS

Not being able to get rid of guilt over time leads to hopelessness. It leaves us resigned to the fact that guilt is just part of life and no matter how painful or heavy our load may be we are stuck with no hope of being rid of it.

SHAME

The last and greatest trap that guilt leads us into is shame. When our guilt defines who we are and what our worth is, we become trapped in shame. Not only can we not free ourselves, not only do we believe that no one else is able to free us, we end up believing that we are not worth saving.

Let me tell you what you already know. You can't get rid of your guilt. You don't have the authority to dismiss it. You don't have the power to remove it. You can't heal the damage it has caused to your soul. We are buried under the rubble of our guilt and we are unable to free ourselves from it.

Now let me tell you what you need to know. God can do what you cannot. Jesus Christ came to make that possible. Here is what you need to know:

If we claim we have no sin, we are only fooling ourselves and not living in the truth. But if we confess our sins to him, he is faithful and just to forgive us our sins and to cleanse us from all wickedness. If we claim we have not sinned, we are calling God a liar and showing that his word has no place in our hearts (1 John 1:8-10).

God can do for you what you cannot do for yourself. What kind of forgiveness is God offering here? Forgiveness for past guilt? Certain kinds of guilt?

God's forgiveness is total. It is forgiveness for everything in the past, forgiveness for the present, and forgiveness for the future. It is total forgiveness, an absolute pardon. That is the only kind of forgiveness that God offers.

What about conditions? What does God require that you do or need to accomplish or promise in order to get this blanket pardon? You need to be honest about your guilt. You need to face it, confess it, and accept that what Jesus did on the cross you are not able to do—pay the price your guilt demanded from God. That's why John says God is just in forgiving us (1 John 1:9). He is not lowering His standards. God is just in His forgiveness. He offers forgiveness to you in Christ because Jesus paid the price God's justice required of you. There is nothing for you to do to earn it. All you need to do is accept it.

What do you need to do to keep it? Once God forgives you, once you take Jesus' offer of forgiveness, He is faithful even when we are not. There is nothing you can do to lose it. There is no sin, there is no person, there is no power that can compete with God's grace.

Sometimes we have a hard time believing that God's grace is for real, and really for us. We worry that our sins and our mistakes might get in the way of God's grace. Chronic feelings of guilt can make you think that you don't deserve God's forgiveness and there is no chance that God is going to waste His grace on you.

No one deserves forgiveness. Grace is not something you can earn like money. Grace is a gift. It can only be accepted. No one deserves forgiveness, but that does not mean God does not offer forgiveness even to the worst sinner. His offer of forgiveness is open to all who will take it regardless of their failures, shortcomings, bad habits, or their amount of guilt. The good news of the gospel is that there is no person so guilty that they cannot lay themselves before the cross of Christ and receive forgiveness.

God's forgiveness removes guilt instantly. If you are struggling with wondering if you have really been forgiven because you still feel guilty—you need to take this to heart. God's forgiveness removes guilt *instantly*. If you have asked God for forgiveness and still feel guilty that does not mean He did not forgive you or that He is punishing you. In *Finding Freedom in Forgiveness* (currently published as *Forgiveness is Tremendous*), Charlie Jones and I wrote,

> While forgiveness is instant, feeling so does not always change that quickly. Even after we are offered forgiveness, often the pain and feeling of guilt linger after the problem has been taken away. One of the biggest reasons for this is that emotions cannot be simply turned on and off at will. The same is true with emotions of anger or hurt. Sometimes even after we forgive we still struggle with anger, resentment and pain.
>
> Our emotions were given to us by God to help us see and understand right and wrong. But sometimes,

because of our sin, they get in the way instead of helping. There is a big qualitative difference between feeling forgiven and actually being forgiven.[14]

There is no sin that God will not forgive. Listen to His promise of forgiveness to you in Psalm 103:8-13: "The LORD is merciful and gracious; he is slow to get angry and full of unfailing love. He will not constantly accuse us, nor remain angry forever. He has not punished us for all our sins, nor does he deal with us as we deserve. For his unfailing love toward those who fear him is as great as the height of the heavens above the earth. He has removed our rebellious acts as far away from us as the east is from the west. The LORD is like a father to his children, tender and compassionate to those who fear him." As the Apostle Paul says in Romans 10:13, "Everyone who calls on the name of the Lord will be saved." Everyone.

Get rid of your guilt. Leave it at the cross. There is no reason to keep carrying it around anymore.

Chapter 10: Rest from Guilt

FREEDOM UNDER SOVEREIGNTY MEANS

Admitting that we all are guilty of falling short of the glory of God (Romans 3:23).

We address our guilt by denying it, burying it, or letting it bury us. But we cannot get rid of it.

God's sovereign grace is the only way to remove our guilt before God.

When we are forgiven by God, our guilt is removed permanently. God no longer looks at us as guilty criminals, but as righteous sons and daughters.

VERSE TO REMEMBER

For there is no other God but me, a righteous God and Savior. There is none but me. Let all the world look to me for salvation! For I am God; there is no other. I have sworn by my own name; I have spoken the truth, and I will never go back on my word.
Isaiah 45:21b-22a

LEARNING TO LIVE UNDER SOVEREIGNTY

1. What are the two ways we can incur guilt? Which do you think people struggle with more?

2. What are some ways that the struggle of guilt can affect people?

3. What does Psalm 103:8-13 say about God's grace? According to this passage, who are the recipients of God's grace?

4. What ways do you see people try to address their feelings of guilt? Have they been successful?

5. It is important to know the difference between being guilty and having feelings of guilt. Why is that?

6. 1 John 1:9 says, "But if we confess our sins to him, he is faithful and just to forgive us our sins and to cleanse us

from all wickedness." How is God just and forgiving at the same time?

7. How have you dealt with your guilt? How might you deal with it differently after reading this chapter?

8. What guilt have you been carrying around in your heart that you need to ask God's forgiveness for?

9. What are one or two things that you can commit to doing to grow your own trust and faith in God's sovereign grace this week?

10. Do you know someone who is struggling with guilt that you might be able to help or pray for? Write their name down and commit to talking to them this week.

CULTIVATING FREEDOM UNDER SOVEREIGNTY

One of the biggest hurdles Christians have who struggle with guilt is that the feeling of guilt lingers on long after they have asked God for forgiveness. One of the confessions I often hear as a pastor is, "I want to believe that God forgave me but I don't feel it at all." Do you know people who have thoughts like that? When people express thoughts like that to me I explain that there is a world of difference between feeling forgiven and being forgiven. When we ask God for forgiveness, He gives it. There is no sin or list of sins that can stain us after we have been bathed in God's gracious forgiveness. How might you explain to someone struggling with guilt that Christ has taken it from them forever and nailed it to the cross?

Memorize and start living out Colossians 3:13, "You must make allowance for each other's faults and forgive the person who offends you. Remember, the Lord forgave you, so you must forgive others."

Study the life of David and see how he dealt with guilt in 1 and 2 Samuel and the Psalms. Specifically look at 2 Samuel

Chapter 10: Rest from Guilt

10-19 and Psalms 38 and 51.

Chapter 11

FREEDOM TO LET GO

No, dear brothers and sisters, I have not achieved it, but I focus on this one thing: Forgetting the past and looking forward to what lies ahead, I press on to reach the end of the race and receive the heavenly prize for which God, through Christ Jesus, is calling us.

PHILIPPIANS 3:13-14

O, I beseech thee, lay hold on this precious thought, perfection in Christ! For thou art "complete in him." With thy Savior's garment on, thou art holy as the Holy one. "Who is he that condemneth? It is Christ that died, yea rather, that is risen again, who is even at the right hand of God, who also maketh intercession for us." Christian, let thy heart rejoice, for thou art "accepted in the beloved"-what hast thou to fear? Let thy face ever wear a smile; live near thy Master; live in the suburbs of the Celestial City; for soon, when thy time has come, thou shalt rise up where thy Jesus sits, and reign at his right hand; and all this because the divine Lord "was made to be sin for us, who knew no sin; that we might be made the righteousness of God in him."

C.H. SPURGEON, *MORNING AND EVENING*,
APRIL 4, MORNING

THE ROAD LESS TRAVELED

I knew the week I was writing this chapter was going to be a busy one for me, so I planned time Monday to work on it in hopes of geting a draft done by the end of the day. By the time 5:00pm rolled around, I had a good draft just about done. I was praising God for his help and insights and illustrations that He brought to my mind. That's when it happened. My computer froze. I lost the whole thing.

I had two choices in front of me. I could complain about how I had lost a whole day's work in an already busy week. Or I could let it go and listen to what God might be trying to communicate to me. I chose the latter. In the words of Robert Frost, "it is the road less traveled by. But those who travel it find it has made all the difference."

ARE YOU A PACK RAT?

Are you the kind of person who likes to hold on to things? My mother-in-law is like that. She holds on to boxes. She had so many boxes that when a friend of mine needed to suddenly pack up and move, she provided all the boxes they needed to move. Even after giving all the boxes they needed she still had boxes left over!

I have a habit of holding onto my notes and papers from college and seminary. I still have them all in file folders in my office. However, I can count on the fingers of one hand how many times I have referred back to them. Yet I can't bring myself to get rid of them.

Many of us have things we like to hold on to. If you are not like this, chances are you know someone who is....you may have even married one! The problem with not wanting to get rid of things is that you start to run out of space after a while. This reality is called "clutter."

Sometimes my office gets so cluttered with things that

need to be put away, given away, or stored away that it becomes difficult for me to find the time or space for the things that need doing.

A few weeks ago I decided it was time to take back my office. That meant letting go of some stuff that I was holding on to. Stuff that (when I got honest with myself) was doing more to keep me disorganized than helping me to be the best pastor I can be. I got rid of three garbage bags full of trash, several dozen books, and some other things that did not need to be in my office. My office is a much more restful and productive space now that I've done that.

SPIRITUAL CLUTTER

There is a spiritual parallel here. Many of us struggle with spiritual clutter. This clutter is made up of the regrets, misgivings, hurts, and failures that make up our past. Even our successes and achievements can become spiritual clutter. We know that we are forgiven of our past in our head but we often have trouble letting it go. We know that God's gracious Spirit can heal us from the wounds and hurts we received in the past, but we often don't experience that. Why?

Simply put, we have a hard time believing the breadth and depth of God's sovereign grace. Listen to how the Apostle Paul deals with his past in light of God's grace in Philippians 3:2-16 (NIV).

> Watch out for those dogs, those people who do evil, those mutilators who say you must be circumcised to be saved. For we who worship by the Spirit of God are the ones who are truly circumcised. We rely on what Christ Jesus has done for us. We put no confidence in human effort, though I could have confidence in my own effort if anyone could.

Indeed, if others have reason for confidence in their own efforts, I have even more! I was circumcised when I was eight days old. I am a pure-blooded citizen of Israel and a member of the tribe of Benjamin—a real Hebrew if there ever was one! I was a member of the Pharisees, who demand the strictest obedience to the Jewish law. I was so zealous that I harshly persecuted the church. And as for righteousness, I obeyed the law without fault.

I once thought these things were valuable, but now I consider them worthless because of what Christ has done. Yes, everything else is worthless when compared with the infinite value of knowing Christ Jesus my Lord. For his sake I have discarded everything else, counting it all as garbage, so that I could gain Christ and become one with him. I no longer count on my own righteousness through obeying the law; rather, I become righteous through faith in Christ. For God's way of making us right with himself depends on faith. I want to know Christ and experience the mighty power that raised him from the dead. I want to suffer with him, sharing in his death, so that one way or another I will experience the resurrection from the dead!

I don't mean to say that I have already achieved these things or that I have already reached perfection. But I press on to possess that perfection for which Christ Jesus first possessed me. No, dear brothers and sisters, I have not achieved it, but I focus on this one thing: Forgetting the past and looking forward to what lies ahead, I press on to reach the end of the race and receive the heavenly prize for which God, through Christ Jesus, is calling us.

Let all who are spiritually mature agree on these things. If you disagree on some point, I believe God will make it plain to you. But we must hold on to the progress we have already made.

Paul reminds us that salvation is by grace and not by works. Salvation is by grace from the beginning to the end. We are saved by works only if they are Christ's works. We rely on what Christ Jesus has done for us. We put no confidence in human effort.

If anyone had reason to boast about his works it was Paul. He could trace his family lineage all the way back to Benjamin, the ultimate father of his tribe. He was named after the greatest Benjaminite in the Bible, King Saul, and was circumcised on the eighth day just as God required in his Law.

Paul was a student of Gamaliel, arguably the greatest Rabbi of his day. Just in order to qualify for such an honor he would have had to be one of the top students of his class and have memorized all 39 books of our Old Testament and have been thoroughly tested in his knowledge and understanding of them in his mid-teens!

He became a Pharisee and his record of keeping the Law even by their strict standards was, humanly speaking, flawless. His zeal became the envy of his fellows. Paul had some fantastic accomplishments and successes in his past that made him stand out among his fellow Israelites.

But Paul had some really bad things in his past too. He was so driven by his zeal for the Law that he was one of the leaders in the Jewish persecution of the Church. He moved against them politically and had them excommunicated from their synagogues, he persecuted them, imprisoned them, and even had them killed. So great was his resolve to wipe the Christians from the face of the earth that Jesus Christ Himself appeared before Him in His heavenly glory, knocked him over, blinded him, and then rebuked him saying, "Saul! Saul! Why are you persecuting me?" I do not think anything less would have gotten his attention!

Can you imagine the guilt he must have felt, realizing that all the work he was doing to fight *for* his God was actually fighting *against* Him? He realized he was responsible for the imprisoning, torturing, and the death of God's own people!

How does Paul deal with his past? He let's it go; both the good and the bad. He lets it all go. Paul says in verses 13 and 14: "I focus on this one thing: Forgetting the past and looking forward to what lies ahead, I press on to reach the end of the race and receive the heavenly prize for which God, through Christ Jesus, is calling us."

Jesus frees us to let go of our past. Let's look at the reason we are free to let go of our past and two reasons why God wants to free us from our past.

WE CAN LET GO OF OUR PAST BECAUSE GOD HAS LET GO OF OUR PAST.

Your past does not in any way influence your position before God. Your position was determined by Christ and Christ alone. When God forgave you He forgave you for everything, no matter how dirty, low, or dark your past might have been. When God accepted you, all the good and wonderful things you have done did not figure into His acceptance of you at all. From the moment we came under grace we became new creatures with new hearts, we became citizens of heaven, co-heirs with Christ with all the rights and privileges of being a brother or sister of Jesus Christ. At that moment God freed us from the tyranny our past. Its power and authority over us was broken.

Someone once said, "The past is valuable as a guidepost, but dangerous if used as a hitching post." God wants us to remember the past so that we learn from it. God wants us to study the Bible and know the Bible which is about the past. All that He wants us to know of Him was written in the past and recorded in the history of Israel and the days of the Apostles. But He does not want us trapped by the past. God has freed us from the past for two reasons.

WE NEED TO LET GO OF OUR PAST SO WE CAN FO-CUS ON OUR WORK FOR TODAY.

When we are focused on the past we can't focus on what we need to be doing today. When the past ceases to be a guidepost and becomes a hitching post, we can't move forward. We become tied down. We are immobilized. When we are fretting about the past we can't be listening to God's voice speaking to us in the present. If we are not giving God our attention, we end up missing the things He wants us to do.

It is dangerous to limit what God is going to do among us and with us based solely on our past. In Isaiah 43:18-19 God said to Israel, "Forget the past! I am doing something new!" Paul tells us that God's sovereign grace can do through us and within us infinitely more than we can ask or even imagine (Ephesians 3:20). But if all we are thinking about is the past, we are kept from having hope in that promise.

WE NEED TO LET GO OF OUR PAST SO THAT WE KEEP OUR FOCUS ON WHERE WE ARE GOING.

A few years ago I was crossing the street on my way back

to my church. When I was halfway across the road I saw a minivan coming that did not seem to see me crossing the street. I started running for the curb, but I was not fast enough. The minivan clipped my leg as I was running by and sent me rolling up onto the sidewalk. Thankfully, the only injury I had was a good-sized raspberry right below my knee where I was hit. Fortunately, the driver stopped. The driver, it turned out, was thinking about an argument that she had earlier in the day with her husband. She admitted that she was preoccupied about that and was not paying attention to the road. When we are focused on our past we aren't looking where we are going. If we are going to be effective servants we need to be making decisions based on where God is taking us and where God is taking His Church. Like Paul, we need to realize the freedom we have in Christ and let go of our past.

WE NEED TO LET GO OF OUR BAD PAST.

You need to let go of the bad things that you have done. I know there are some of you reading this who struggle with regret and guilt over your past: failures, poor decisions, and times you stood by and did nothing when you knew you needed to act. Others of you reading this are struggling with a past of pain that others inflicted on you: abuse, betrayal, being laid off or fired, illness, or the loss of a loved one.

God wants you to know that it is OK to grieve your hurts. It is healthy to have remorse for our sins. There is no prescribed timetable for getting over a tragedy or hurt or loss. Whoever said "time heals all wounds" was an idiot! I still have pangs of regret and feel the wounds I have received for hurts long gone by. But by the grace of God, you can have the poison of those times taken from your wounds.

God's grace has already cleansed you from your guilt. You are free to let go. God has promised to bind your wounds and heal them, there is no wound so deep He cannot heal. No anger He cannot drain. We need to take a walk to the cross where we see it all nailed where Jesus was. Your guilt was paid for at the cross. You can let it go. Your anger was answered by God at the cross, His justice acted on your behalf there. You can let it go.

Were you abandoned? So was Jesus. Were you abused? So was He. Have you been betrayed? So was He. Have you felt confined? So has He. Jesus wants you to stop beating yourself up about the past. He wants you to stop fretting over what happened, what didn't happen, what should have happened, and what could have happened. He wants you to let it all go so you can hold onto Him, so you can see that His arms are still holding you tight. Let go so you can hold on to Him.

WE NEED TO LET GO OF OUR GOOD PAST.

Does that surprise you? It is just as important to let go of your good past as it is to let go of your bad past. When you start to place your confidence in what you have done, you put yourself in the place where you start depending on Christ less.

Paul found himself in this position. He thought that obeying the Law and doing good works was the basis for God's approval of him. He achieved a level of success in that regard that few people have. But when he met Christ he realized how wrong he had been. He said, "I once thought these things were valuable, but now I consider them worthless because of what Christ has done. Yes, everything else is worthless when compared with the infinite value of knowing Christ Jesus my Lord."

Yesterday's successes are meant to give us confidence that God will bless us today. Jesus said, "I am the vine; you are the branches. Those who remain in me, and I in them, will produce much fruit. For apart from me you can do nothing" (John 15:5). You can do a lot of things by yourself, but you can't do anything for God by yourself. Our successes need to be growing our faith in God's grace, not increasing our own pride. We need to let go of our successes, our achievements, our victories, because they were never ours in the first place. They were His.

Let go of your bad past. God has cleared you of your guilt. It is gone. It no longer exists. Your slate has been wiped clean. You are free.

Let go of your good past and avoid the trap of pride in your own accomplishments. God's grace is sufficient for you. You do not need to earn your place. It was given to you by grace. You are free to forget the past and look forward to what lies ahead, so that you can press on to reach the end of the race and receive the heavenly prize for which God, through Christ Jesus, is calling us.

We can stop worrying that grace is going to run out. We can admit our mistakes, failings, and shortcomings. They don't define who we are. We can learn from the past instead of languishing in the past. We don't have to worry about failing, and falling. We can let go of hurts that others have done to us. God paid for it at the cross. There is no debt remaining to be paid.

FREEDOM UNDER SOVEREIGNTY MEANS

Salvation is by grace from the beginning to the end. We are saved by works only if they are Christ's works.

Your past does not in any way influence your position before God.

When we are fretting about the past we can't be listening to God's voice speaking to us in the present. When we are focused on our past we aren't looking where we are going.

God wants you to stop fretting over your bad past: what happened, what didn't happen, what should have happened, and what could have happened. He wants you to let it all go so you can hold onto Him.

Let go of your good past and avoid the trap of pride in your own accomplishments.

VERSE TO REMEMBER

No, dear brothers and sisters, I have not achieved it, but I focus on this one thing: Forgetting the past and looking forward to what lies ahead, I press on to reach the end of the race and receive the heavenly prize for which God, through Christ Jesus, is calling us.
Philippians 3:13-14

LEARNING TO LIVE UNDER SOVEREIGNTY

1. Read Philippians 3:2-16. What accomplishments does Paul claim for himself? What does he think about them? What is the reason for bringing up such an impressive list of successes and achievements? What is the point Paul is making in this passage?

2. Do you know someone who like Paul believed what they were doing was what God wanted only to discover that they were acting against Him?

3. Do you know anyone who has spiritual clutter? If so,

what are some examples of things that might be labeled spiritual clutter?

4. What do you think Paul means by saying, "Forgetting the past and looking forward to what lies ahead"? Are we supposed to forget what happened to us in the past?

5. Why is Paul so confident that his past does not add or subtract from his relationship with God though Jesus Christ?

6. How can remembering our past be harmful? How can remembering our past be helpful?

7. Is there something in your past that has become a hitching post to you? What can you apply from this chapter to help you transform that hitching post into a guidepost?

8. Why is it just as important to let go of your good past as it is to let go of your bad past?

9. What keeps you from completely letting go of your past so that you can live in the freedom of Christ's grace, forgiveness, and blessing?

10. What is one thing you can commit to doing this week to increase your trust in God's sovereign grace?

Cultivating Freedom Under Sovereignty

Focusing on our past mistakes can make us so afraid that we can't hear God's voice of direction. Just as serious, focusing on past successes can foster pride that keeps us from hearing God's voice as well. When I make a mistake, I own it and ask for forgiveness. Then I ask what God wants me to be learning from that mistake. I am very slow to talk about my successes or achievements. One of the things I do to keep my educational achievements from building up pride is by insisting that people at my church call me "Dan." Not "Pastor Dan," not "Reverend Ledwith," just "Dan." What are some things you can do to keep fear and pride from your past from keeping you focused on what God wants you doing in the present?

You can help yourself and those around you let go of their past by being quick to forgive. Write down anyone you might be holding a grudge against or that you might have hurt and offer forgiveness.

One of the things I have done and counseled others to do who have trouble giving their past to God is to write down on a piece of paper whatever about their past might be keeping them from focusing on God's grace in the present. Then tell God you are sending these things to Him and ask Him to help you let go of your past. Then burn the paper, symbolizing that God has taken it from you.

THE NEXT STEP

In a previous church, I wrote a regular column in the church newsletter called *What I've Been Learning.* The title was very deliberate. Not "what I've *learned"* but "what I've been *learning."* My friend Charlie Jones said, "When someone says 'you know what I've learned' you know what they've learned? Nothing!" I used to say "you know what I've learned" too, but then I began realizing that the thing I was learning this week was the thing I said I had learned the week before! Now I realize, along with Charlie Jones, that I haven't learned much, but I've been learning a whole lot!

You have started on a journey learning about the sovereignty of God that is going to have huge benefits for the rest of your life. In reading this book you have been given a lot of knowledge about God's sovereignty and how it impacts how we think and act in light of God's promises every day.

One day I was sitting in the car with my dad having a coffee when I got a call from the church. One of our Stephen Ministers was there with a man who was saying he wanted to slit his wrists.

I went right to the church. On the way I prayed for discernment, insight, wisdom, and grace. I asked God to have people pray for me. I asked for God to be with the Stephen Minister and with the man she was with. When I arrived at the church, I went in with the confidence that God had heard my prayers and answered them and would give me all I needed to help this person.

When I got there the man and the Stephen Minister were sitting on a couch.

"My name is Dan," I said. "what's your name?"

"David."

"Nice to meet you." I said, and sat down next to him. "How are you?"

"I'm scared. I want to cut myself."

"Why would you want to do that?"

Our conversation went on for a few minutes. God gave me wisdom to ask questions that helped me to understand him, where he had come from and what his mental state was.

"Do you have a knife?"

"Yeah."

"Would you give it to me?"

"Aren't you afraid of me?"

"No."

Dave started to reach into his pocket. "You're not afraid of me?"

"No, I'm not afraid of you. I want to help you. Give me your knife."

"I'm afraid. I just want to die. Kill me."

"No. I won't do that. Do you know what? The Bible says that 'Our God is in the heavens and He does whatever He pleases.' Do you believe that?"

"Yeah."

"That means God wanted to make you. You bring God pleasure. You are important to Him. And that means you are important to me. God loved you enough to bring Jan and me into your life. God does not want you to kill yourself. He loves you too much, that's why we're here. You probably think that you have nothing to live for and no one will care or even notice if you are gone. Maybe that was true yesterday, but today you know that I care, that Jan cares, and that God cares about you and what happens to you."

But actually applying these truths to our marriage, family, church, finances, work, and friends is going to be a lot of work. Don't be discouraged!

Focus on one promise a month so that in a year you will have gone through each of the promises.

It is one thing to know these promises. It is another to live in them. Focus on them. Pray about them. Memorize them.

GOD IS SOVEREIGN: PSALM 115:3

For our God is in the heavens, and he does as he wishes.

FREEDOM FROM DEPRESSION: JEREMIAH 29:11

For I know the plans I have for you," says the LORD. "They are plans for good and not for disaster, to give you a future and a hope.

FREEDOM FROM GUILT: ISAIAH 45:21-22

For there is no other God but me—a just God and a Savior—no, not one! Let all the world look to me for salvation! For I am God; there is no other.

FREEDOM FROM ANXIETY: JOHN 14:14

Yes, ask anything in my name, and I will do it!

FREEDOM FROM FEAR: DEUTERONOMY 31:6

Be strong and courageous! Do not be afraid of them! The LORD your God will go ahead of you. He will neither fail you nor forsake you.

FREEDOM FROM SHAME: PSALM 34:5

Those who look to him for help will be radiant with joy;

no shadow of shame will darken their faces.

FREE TO ENJOY: 1 PETER 1:8

You love him even though you have never seen him. Though you do not see him, you trust him; and even now you are happy with a glorious, inexpressible joy.

FREE TO LET GO: PHILIPPIANS 3:13-14

No, dear brothers and sisters, I am still not all I should be, but I am focusing all my energies on this one thing: Forgetting the past and looking forward to what lies ahead, I strain to reach the end of the race and receive the prize for which God, through Christ Jesus, is calling us up to heaven.

FREE TO HOPE: ROMANS 15:13

May the God of hope fill you with all joy and peace in believing, so that by the power of the Holy Spirit you may abound in hope.

FREE TO LIVE BOLDLY: PROVERBS 28:1

The wicked run away when no one is chasing them, but the godly are as bold as lions.

FREE TO LOVE: JEREMIAH 31:3

Long ago the LORD said to Israel: "I have loved you, my people, with an everlasting love. With unfailing love I have drawn you to myself.

LEARNING TO BE DEPENDENT

One of the main lessons God wants us to be learning is dependence on Him. He wants us learning how much we need to depend on Him. We cannot be depending on ourselves. We like to think that we are able to handle ourselves most of the time, as if we only need God's grace and provision for certain things or at certain times. The truth is we need Him all the time. God deliberately brings things into our lives to humble us and wake us up to how blind we are, how weak we are, and how helpless we are. He will send things to drive us to our knees so that we come to Him in prayer. We often act like the prodigal son and take the blessings we have been given and attempt to live life on our own terms. But like the prodigal son we will come to the point where we realize that we need Him. He wants us learning how much we can depend on Him.

Once God begins to wake us up to our need for Him, He then begins to show us just how much we can trust Him. No matter how great the need, no matter how far we fall, no matter how deeply we bury ourselves, God can provide for us, lift us up, and carry us out of whatever pit we are in. God wants you to know that He is sovereign. He is all powerful. His goodness guides everything in your life to work for your joy and His glory. His grace can clean you from any amount of guilt you have. Generosity will provide for all your needs. His faithfulness assures that He will never leave you or forsake you. His love can wipe away any shame you have.

Living in the freedom of Christ's promises means learning to rest in the truth of God's sovereignty. His sovereignty guarantees that what Christ died to purchase for you, you will be given.

Get free. Get free from your past. Get free from your guilt. Get free from anxiety about tomorrow. Get free from fear about today. Get free from depression over the difficulties you have. God's love means freedom. Freedom to live a life full of joy, to let go of your past, to have hope for the future, to live boldly, and to love passionately with the same love God has for you. Get free. Be free.

INDEX

END NOTES

[1] Jonathan Edwards, *Works of Jonathan Edwards, Volume 1, Freedom of the Will*, ed. Paul Ramsey (New Haven, Yale University Press, 1957), pp. 378-380.

[2] This story is from an unnamed source in Sermon Builder 4.0.

[3] http://www.catholiceducation.org/articles/abortion/ab0039.html.

[4] Jonathan Edwards, *A Watchman's Concern for Souls* in *Works of Jonathan Edwards, Volume 25, Sermons and Discourses, 1743-1758*, Ed. Wilson H. Kimnach Works, JE 25, p. 64. Hereafter cited as "WJE 25."

[5] WJE 25, p. 65.

[6] Ibid.

[7] Unattributed illustration from *Heart Warming Bible Illustrations*, Sermon Builders 4.0.

[8] Jonathan Edwards, *Charity and Its Fruits, in Works of Jonathan Edwards, Volume 8, Ethical Writings,* ed. Paul Ramsey (New Haven, Yale University Press, 1989), p. 254. Hereafter cited as "WJE 8."

[9] WJE 8, p. 254.

[10] WJE 8, pp. 254-255.

[11] WJE 8, p. 258.

[12] WJE 8, p. 263.

[13] *USA Today* (1/4/99) source: Yankelovich Monitor. *Leadership*, Vol. 20, no. 3.

[14] Charlie Jones and Daniel R. Ledwith, *Finding Freedom in Forgiveness*, (Eugene, Harvest House Publishers, 2005), pp. 94-95.